Joseph McCabe

Modern rationalism

Joseph McCabe

Modern rationalism

ISBN/EAN: 9783743335745

Manufactured in Europe, USA, Canada, Australia, Japa

Cover: Foto ©ninafisch / pixelio.de

Manufactured and distributed by brebook publishing software (www.brebook.com)

Joseph McCabe

Modern rationalism

MODERN RATIONALISM.

BEING

A SKETCH OF THE

PROGRESS OF THE RATIONALISTIC SPIRIT IN THE NINETEENTH CENTURY.

BY

JOSEPH McCABE.

LONDON:
WATTS & CO., 17, JOHNSON'S COURT, FLEET St.

1897.

CONTENTS.

INTRODUCTION	5
CHAPTER I.—RATIONALISM IN THEOLOGY	15
CHAPTER II.—BIBLICAL CRITICISM	44
CHAPTER III.—COMPARATIVE RELIGION AND MYTHOLOGY	81
CHAPTER IV.—RATIONALISM AND PHILOSOPHY	104
CHAPTER V.—RELIGION AND SCIENCE	123
CHAPTER VI.—RATIONALISM IN ETHICS; CONSTRUCTIVE RATIONALISM	149

INTRODUCTION.

RATIONALISM is a term of such diverse connotations in the minds of different writers that, like the term "Socialism," it is not susceptible of any brief definition which should be free from ambiguity. The intellectual method, or attitude, or spirit which is suggested by it has inspired such heterogeneous systems in the controversial struggle of the last few centuries that it can no longer be said to describe any actual system with clearness. It is applied equally to Agnosticism, the extreme revolutionary form of heterodoxy, and to a certain theological school that professes to remain within the precincts of the orthodox temple; and it is frequently taken to be synonymous with a destructive system of Biblical criticism. Rationalism, in the earlier part of the last century, was a school of anti-Christian Deists in England and France; towards the close of the century, and in the earlier part of the present century, it was a system of Biblical criticism, usually of a hostile character; *modern* Rationalism is a system which rejects both natural and supernatural theology, and is antagonistic to the orthodox Churches on every point, although the term is still often used in its earlier senses.

However, it is easy to trace through all these systems, divergent and even contradictory as they would have been if they had co-existed, the operation of one and the same spirit. The Deist rejected supernatural religion, but emphatically retained belief in a personal God; whereas the modern Rationalist declines all profession of a Theistic nature—or, at the most, retains only a profession of the most evanescent character. Yet the principle which actuated the departure from orthodoxy was the same in both cases: it was discovered to have a deeper application by the later generation. Both schools, and indeed all systems to which the name is applied, accepted as their primary and fundamental principle that *reason* is the supreme criterion of all truth, whether in secular or religious, natural or supernatural, spheres. Any thesis, on whatever authority it may be asserted, which violates the dictates of reason must be rejected. On that test were rejected, first the mysterious rites and dogmas of Christianity, then its sacred literature, and, finally, even the positions of natural theology. From Collins and Shaftesbury to Mill and Huxley the history of Rationalism is but a consistent and progressive application of that principle.

Rationalism, therefore, is rather a "cast of thought" and "bias of reasoning," as Mr. Lecky says, than a stereotyped system, although he would seem to define it inadequately in saying that "its central conception is the elevation of conscience into a position of supreme authority as the religious organ, a verifying faculty discriminating between truth and error;" for *speculative* reason has been as operative as *practical* reason in the destructive progress of Rationalism. From all time there have been religious statements current among all nations which purported to come from a source other than the natural activity of the human mind, from a higher authority, and before which the vast majority of mankind have bent in feeble and unquestioning submission. Sooner or later, however, a departure from that attitude is inevitable. Reason claims its prerogative as the ultimate test of all truth, applies its first principles and the knowledge it has already acquired to all ethical and religious traditions, and comes to reject a greater or less section, or even the whole, of its inherited profession.

Unless, however, this activity of reason yields conspicuous

destructive results, it does not attract the title of Rationalism. Thus, even the Church of Rome, most conservative of orthodox sects, recognises that reason is a tribunal from which there is no appeal (it is one of the first propositions of dogmatic theology); yet the title of "Rationalistic" was not applied until the school of Günther and Hermes (which was promptly suppressed) began to alter its stereotyped formulæ. So, also, in the Church of England (and Germany) only that school is called Rationalistic which departs in a marked degree, in dogma or Biblical criticism, from the formulæ which have been sanctioned by the religious acceptance of many centuries, and which constitute what may safely be called orthodoxy. The Rationalistic spirit is, therefore, a critical action of reason on authoritative religious tradition, which leads to its partial or entire rejection, either from defect of satisfactory evidence to recommend it, or because it conflicts with known facts or evident moral or speculative principles—the negative and positive criterion of the Catholic theologian.

The importance of that spirit in the modern world of thought cannot be exaggerated. Mr. Lecky states that it "seems absolutely to over-ride our age." Yet it must not be supposed to be an exclusively modern phenomenon; in every civilized nation there are manifestations of it from the earliest dawn of scientific thought. Reason has ever protested, in its nobler embodiments, against the excessive tyranny of authority and the excessive credulity of the majority. At least, in such nations as had a body of cultured laymen, distinct from the sacerdotal body, it led to the formation of powerful antagonistic systems. In Greece, which enjoyed that prerogative to an extent which has found a parallel only in the modern civilized world, speculation had the utmost freedom, and was indulged without a glance at the religious traditions of the race. From Thales to Carneades a marvellous diversity of systems crossed the intellectual arena, the majority of them freely modifying and combating the most fundamental points of tradition. At Rome there was less originality, but equal liberty and scepticism, when the great military nation found time at length for culture and reflection; all educated Romans were Stoics or Neo-Academic sceptics. In Judæa the Rationalistic spirit found emphatic expression in the Sadducees, who denied the most essential points of traditional belief—even the immortality of the soul.

And from the very commencement of the Christian era the spirit manifests itself in revolt. The Gnostics attempted a curious blending of Oriental mysticism and Platonic philosophy applied to Christianity. The great Trinitarian struggles of the fourth and fifth centuries were due to its operation. Even within the Church, at Alexandria, the then centre of the intellectual world, a semi-Rationalism was evolved, which culminated in the περι αρχων of Origen. A continuous series of heresiarchs illustrate it until the twelfth century, some of whom, as John Scotus Erigena, the celebrated Irish scholar of the tenth century, professed scepticism on the most fundamental points, such as the fire of hell and even the personal existence of the Deity. In the twelfth century the fierce renewal of intellectual life developed much Rationalism. Abelard seems to have been a typical, though a timid, free-thinker, and made a strenuous effort to disentangle philosophy from theology. At the same time, Rationalism of a profound character was brought to bear upon the theological world from the Arab schools in Spain. So powerful was their influence, indeed, that Averroes came to be identified with Antichrist. Even among the pious schoolmen there were Rationalists. Joannes Paulus de Oliva cowardly retracted his teaching. Scotus was a semi-Rationalist; his English pupil, Occam, a thorough Rationalist, who boldly rejected the authority of the Church. In the fifteenth century the immigration of the Greeks to Italy after the fall of Constantinople led to a splendid revival of Greek art and literature. A freethought movement, culminating in Pomponatius (1462–1524), was very powerful in the universities of Padua and Bologna, and philosophy once more made an effort to speculate apart from theology. But the Church was still all-powerful; it crushed the Renaissance which it had at first patronized.

In the sixteenth century came the great revolt against the time-honoured authority of the Church, which effectively prepared the way for the marvellous development of Rationalism in the last three centuries. The reformers, indeed, extended little patronage to the exercise of reason in religious matters; they denounced it and its fruit, philosophical speculation, as an evil not to be tolerated; and Luther went so far as to assert (even to the disgust of the Church of Rome) that a proposition may be true in theology and false in philosophy. Still, by the force of their own example, they inevitably introduced the Rationalistic spirit, the right of personal speculation on authoritative teaching: when the impressiveness of their usurped authority waned, the practical lesson of their revolt, the right to examine and criticise, was more clearly perceived. At the same time, no adequate and permanent authority was established in place of the rejected papacy; an admittedly fallible authority only encourages criticism and individual speculation. The iron bond of unity and discipline was broken, never to be replaced; no authority remained that could absolutely enforce a devised formula, and against which revolt would have a supernatural demerit. A Church teaching in virtue of its collective wisdom, and expounding an obscure objective code of faith and morals, could never hope to repress individual vagaries.

Other causes co-operated happily in hastening the dawn of perfect liberty of thought. The rapid multiplication of sects and dissipation of spiritual jurisdiction made it possible for independent thinkers to escape a persecuting authority and take up a bold, isolated position. Culture, too, began to pass more extensively into the ranks of the laity, who were naturally more ready to express their scepticism than the professional theological caste. Secular sciences, history, and physics began to breathe freely at last and develop in utter disregard of religious doctrines. Printing was introduced; a religious controversy thus obtained an infinitely wider audience than it had had formerly, and the writings of sceptics were universally diffused. The destruction of a venerable authority, the violent changes of theological schemes, the deafening roar of controversy, the accumulation of diverse and contradictory opinions, tended to produce distrust in the educated and bewilderment in the uneducated. Such, briefly, were the predisposing conditions of modern Rationalism.

One important Rationalistic school, Socinianism, the revival of Arianism, and predecessor of modern Unitarianism, dates from the time of the Reformation itself. Still, it is only attributable to the Reformation in the sense that that movement afforded it some liberty of utterance and expansion. It may easily be traced through the Italian-Greeks of the Renaissance to the earlier Greek heresy ; if, indeed, it may not be said to voice the unceasing impatience of the mind in all ages under the Christian mysteries, especially the dogma of the Trinity. This time, however, the system came to stay, and it has played a most important part in the rationalization of theology. But the broader Rationalistic movement soon began in earnest with the appearance of isolated writers of great authority, of enduring influence, and often of the most destructive scepticism. In 1588 Montaigne published the first great sceptical work of a thoroughly Pyrrhonist character. A literary critic of profound influence, he was in effect a Rationalist of the most advanced type ; his essays were the inauguration of the modern period of Freethought. He was warmly supported by Charron, a French priest, and is even said to have profoundly influenced Pascal. Descartes also, with his system of philosophic doubt, assisted the growth of freedom and reflection. Bayle was not only profoundly sceptical in the composition of his *Dictionary*, but he made a most eloquent and effective appeal in smaller works, as the *Compelle Intrare*, for liberty of thought and expression. Even the religious Leibnitz earned the title of "Glöbenichts" (believer of nothing). Spinoza was profoundly destructive.

In England a series of powerful writers embodied the Rationalistic spirit with great effect in the seventeenth and eighteenth centuries. Bacon had virtually commenced the movement with his protest against "idols" and authority and the insistence on an empirical method. Hobbes followed with a most uncompromising iconoclasm. Locke introduced the empiric philosophy, which is so largely responsible for the Agnosticism of the nineteenth century. Hume developed the system and indicated its true conclusion, and diffused a literary scepticism with far-reaching effect. Gibbon brought the Rationalistic spirit to bear on history. If it is true that "the controversialists of successive ages are the puppets and unconscious exponents of the deep under-currents of their time," the Rationalistic spirit must have made rapid progress in England since the rejection of Papal despotism. One salutary effect of the controversies and of the downfall of Rome was the birth of a spirit of toleration for the first time in the history of Christianity; even orthodox writers, such as Chillingworth (the first to do so), began to teach "the absolute innocence of error."

In the course of the eighteenth century the controversy assumed a different character. Rationalistic criticism passed from the contents of Christianity to its external defences; the spirit was penetrating deeper every century. There was, it is true, a fierce revival of the Trinitarian controversy. The Unitarians waxed bolder and stronger in their attempt to rationalize theology, and some of their Trinitarian opponents, headed by Bull and Waterland, developed a semi-Rationalism on their own side, dropping off, as in the ancient controversy, into semi-Arianism on the one side, and Tritheism on the other. But the struggle is principally characterized by the rise of the Deistic school. Allied with the Voltairean school, which was permeating France with Rationalism, there was in England a powerful body of writers—Toland, Collins (the first to bear the title of Freethinker), Chubb, Woolston, Tindal, Shaftesbury, and Bolingbroke, who made a virulent organized attack upon the very credentials of Christianity, ridiculing its history and its mysterious contents, and denying the very possibility of miracles. They were opposed by Dr. S. Clarke, Dr. Berkeley, and Dr. Butler (the first two again developing a certain amount of private Rationalism in the course of their apologetic efforts). The rise and spread of Wesleyanism created a diversion in favour of the Rationalists by slighting the efforts of the evidential school and creating an emotional concentration upon the Atonement and similar doctrines. The fall of High-Churchism and the ascendancy of the Broad Church tended to produce a similar effect. Still, it is not too much to say that the Deistic controversy remains buried in the eighteenth century. As a consecration and development of the Rationalistic spirit, the Deistic school wrought an enduring effect. But even the brilliant writings of Bolingbroke and Shaftesbury are now practically shelved. Hume and Gibbon are the only Rationalists whose works pass on into the nineteenth century.

Such had been the progress of the Rationalistic spirit up to the period with which this sketch will deal. As a spirit, or method, it had been extensively used against orthodox belief; but few of its results were useful in the great struggle of the present century. The controversy once more changes its entire character, though animated by the same spirit. Modern Rationalism differs in two ways from Voltairean or Deistic Rationalism. It is more fundamental, and it is not merely destructive, but teaches also elevated social and ethical ideals to humanity. Once the spirit of criticism had successfully attacked the evidences of supernatural religion, it turned its attention to the evidences of natural religion, or pure Theism, which the older Rationalists had respected.

The century opens with a development of the empirical philosophy which rapidly produces its most negative results. Coleridge introduces the transcendental philosophy from Germany, which he has learned from Kant's followers, and the first efforts of Biblical criticism from Lessing and Semler. In the course of the century the empirical philosophy developes into pure Agnosticism and Positivism, evokes a brilliant series of exponents from James Mill to Spencer, and obtains a wide acceptance from the gradually-educated country. German philosophy runs its course into Hegelian Pantheism, and its moral anxiety, in virtue of which it still clung to Theism, finds a relief in the rise and rapid growth of a system of purely rational ethics. Biblical criticism, availing itself of the growing effectiveness of philology and archæology, works a revolution in the educated and the popular view of the Bible. Physical science makes gigantic progress throughout the century, rising like a flood over the successive entrenchments of retreating theologians, and constructing a new view of man and his material environment, which induces a profound modification of the earlier theological teaching. History throws new and wondrous light upon the origin and nature and ethical contents of non-Christian religions, and the strange analogy of their myths to Christian dogmas. Education is improved and secularized; the spirit of inquiry pervades the masses. By the end of the century a sceptical Rationalism "absolutely over-rides our age,"* and "is found in every able book" which we open. The list of ardent Rationalists in England

---

* Lecky's "History of the Rise and Influence of the Spirit of Rationalism."

includes the two Mills, Darwin, Lewes, Spencer, Carlyle, George Eliot, Arnold, Shelley, the two Stephens, Huxley, Tyndall, Morley, Lyell, Bain, Max Müller, Lecky, Browning, Tennyson, Tylor, Lubbock, Clifford, F. Harrison, Sully, Maudsley, and Bastian. The vast majority are Rationalists of extreme type, or Agnostics.

At the same time a change has been taking place within the orthodox Church itself. The ceaseless attack of ethical and speculative criticism upon its dogmas has had a profound corrosive influence. The clear lines that were laid down in the ecclesiastical conscience have grown dim and shadowy: several specific dogmas have been completely transformed, works of quite a revolutionary character have emanated from professed theologians, and there has been a general tendency to attach more importance to ethical and useful conduct, and much less to creeds and formulæ. Biblical criticism and comparative religion have also deeply affected theological positions. This rationalizing tendency *inside* the Church may be described before proceeding to more fundamental changes.

MODERN RATIONALISM.

Chapter I.

RATIONALISM IN THEOLOGY.

"The surrender to infidelity by the so-called Christian minister is the most alarming feature of the hour" are words which an eminent American preacher of the Evangelical school addressed to his congregation a few years ago. The words are true, with an apology for the crudity of the expression, not only of America, but of England, Germany, Holland, France, and Switzerland. Though it is scarcely correct to speak of this Rationalistic tendency as merely a feature of the present hour: it is one of the most interesting features of the century as a whole, and has, in our days, come to be accepted as a permanent phenomenon. There were, it is true, occasional indications of the same spirit in the preceding century. Dr. Berkeley constructed a philosophical system, which, if fully evolved, would have grave theological consequences; and Dr. Clarke even called himself humorously "a freethinking anti-Freethinker." Still, there was no evidence of a systematic effort to elevate reason or conscience to the dignity of arbiter of all truth, including revealed, and to deliberately modify or reject under its influence some of the most essential points of Christian doctrine. But at the very commencement of the nineteenth century that spirit reveals its operation. A powerful school is formed within the Church under its inspiration which makes such rapid progress that, in 1833, the thoughtful and anxious Newman, in the van of the opposing Tractarian movement, declared that "the nation was on its way to give up revealed truth." Since that date it has steadily grown, and has come at length to be accepted as a legitimate school within the Church; and legal enactments have been especially framed to accommodate it.

Thus, side by side with the growth of Unitarianism and the rise and progress of Agnosticism, the Rationalistic spirit has penetrated into ecclesiastical circles and caused an interesting internal struggle. The history of the Broad Church, as the rationalizing section has been called since Mr. Conybeare's article, is an important chapter in the history of Rationalism, and its significance, in conjecturing the ultimate issue of the conflict of reason and authority, is very profound. For the present it has had the effect of preserving the numerical strength of the Established Church; it has been found a most effective safety-valve under hostile pressure. Since that effect has only been attained by an important sacrifice and the admission of the very spirit which has raised up inimical bodies, it is probable that there will be further interesting developments. Private judgment in the seventeenth century became, by a logical evolution, Deism in the eighteenth century and Agnosticism in the nineteenth. What is likely to be the evolution of Christian Rationalism?

The influences which have engendered and nourished that rationalizing and concessive tendency are numerous and complex, and, on the whole, peculiar outcomes of the present marvellous century. Two different schools of philosophy, one of German origin and the other a development of the sensism of Locke and Hume, have had a large share in producing it. The astonishing progress of physical science, and its exposure of many quasi-religious traditions, has had a great influence. The vivid light which has been thrown upon non-Christian and pre-Christian religions, the saner reconstruction of the history of Christianity itself, the elaboration of an ethical system on an exclusively humanitarian basis, and especially the flood of light which has been thrown on Christian sacred literature, are other important factors in the development. All these have been operative in the growth of all kinds of Rationalism; but the influence which may be peculiarly associated with the growth of Rationalism in theology is the candid application of reason, both moral and speculative, to the doctrines of traditional Christianity in themselves. The history of this influence is the history of the Broad Church of the Anglican Establishment which we trace in this chapter.

In the eighteenth century English Rationalism had been allied with France. At the great Revolution that alliance ceased, and much hostility was shown to the Deistic tenets which were considered to have brought on the politcial trouble in France. The noble and strenuous figure of Paine lingers on the threshold of the nineteenth century, amid a storm of calumny and persecution, as the last representative of the old school. After his imprisonment by the Republic for interference on behalf of the unfortunate king, he returned to England and met with a fierce hostility on publishing his "Age of Reason;" in fact, as late as 1819, Richard Carlile was sentenced to three years' imprisonment and £1,500 fine for publishing it. Paine returned to America in 1802, and the old form of Rationalism only survived, as a system and with modifications, in Unitarianism.

English scholars then began to seek in Germany that original thought of which England seemed barren and Germany was then especially prolific. Among them was one who was destined to be the founder of the Broad Church, Samuel Taylor Coleridge. "Ever since that profound thinker assumed a fixed position," says Hurst, "a re-action against orthodoxy has been progressing in the Established Church;" and J. Mill calls him one of our chief "seminal" thinkers. Coleridge was already imbued with a culture which effectively predisposed to liberal speculation. At Christ's Hospital and at Cambridge he had been an ardent Hellenist, and had familiarized himself with Plato, and afterwards with the Alexandrian philosophy and theology—the idealistic school of the early Church. He went to Germany in 1798, and attached himself to the philosophy of Kant. For a time he was converted to Hegel; but, dreading the Pantheistic element of Hegel's teaching, he returned to Kant. With the speculations of the Alexandrian Greeks and the principles of the "religion within the limits of reason" acting on his own poetical temperament, his theological opinions soon began to undergo a transformation.

When he returned to England he began at once to introduce German literature to his countrymen; he and De Quincey were the first English interpreters of German thought. The prevailing heresy at home at that period was Benthamism, and to this Coleridge opposed the idealized and somewhat mystic form of Christianity which he had now conceived. The High Church form of Anglicanism had been steadily declining since the seventeenth century; and the Low Church, less mindful of rites and formulæ, had gained considerable ground. Methodism, too, had earnestly propagated the habit of attaching more importance to morals than to speculations and the technicalities of theology. Hence, perhaps, Coleridge found a not unwilling soil and less hostility; yet his teaching was certainly conspicuously novel. His freedom of thought is seen particularly in his treatment of sin, especially original sin. He does not admit that it is guilt in the orthodox sense, hence he is led to more lenient thoughts of its punishment. Adam, he says, merely incurs God's displeasure by his act, and is stripped of his supernatural gifts; the *sin* which his descendants inherit is nothing more grievous—they are left to their natural condition. Redemption, therefore, does not mean salvation from the curse of a broken law, and Christ cannot be said to have paid a debt for man, because no positive debt had been incurred. Still, he removed God's displeasure and reconciled humanity to him. In later life Coleridge is said to have been a sincere Trinitarian, but he had planted the seeds of many heresies in his new scheme.

It was through Julius Hare principally that the new doctrine was propagated. Hare was a Fellow of Trinity College, Cambridge, and he soon formed a powerful school of adherents to the new doctrine, of which the most conspicuous members were John Sterling, F. D. Maurice, and Trench. Each, as usually happens, evolved some personal notions, but the general principles on sin and the atonement remain unchanged. Hare takes a new view of sacrifice; says that Christ did not execute his important mission so much by his death as by his entire life—his example. Sin is a matter rather of regret than of responsibility. Miracles have been wrongly considered a necessary support of Christianity; they are rather a decoration of its structure, which stands by its moral worth. Scripture contains many verbal inaccuracies. Faith is not an active force, and, *per se*, a source of merit; it is rather a passive endowment. Such was the teaching which resounded in the halls of Trinity early in the century.

Maurice, also, is latitudinarian with regard to Scripture. He regards its ethical contents principally, and is prepared to yield on questions of form. Sin is nothing more than a certain condition of our life. It is not guilt or responsibility, not a consequence of actual disobedience of God's law or an effect of his displeasure. Christ was not a mediatorial substitute for humanity, but its natural representative with the Father. From his peculiar view of physical death, it followed that there could be no resurrection or general judgment in the orthodox sense. Maurice occupied the chair of Divinity at King's College, London, and for some time after the publication of his "Essays" no notice was taken of his heterodoxy. At length the principal, Dr. Jelf, was induced to read them, and he at once, in 1853, took steps for the removal of Maurice. He, however, still continued in the Anglican ministry, and was for some time chaplain to Lincoln's Inn, and after a few years was appointed by the Queen's authority to the district church of Vere Street, Marylebone. Finally, in 1866, he was appointed to a chair of Moral Philosophy at Cambridge.

In the same connection must be mentioned Kingsley, who disseminated the new liberalism in a series of brilliant novels. Having had Derwent Coleridge, son of Samuel Taylor, for tutor, he was early attracted to the new movement. The atonement he, like his predecessors, denied to be a reconciliation of sinful humanity with an angry deity. Christianity was not a remedial dispensation, but only an outward exhibition of the union of humanity with God that had always existed. Christ did not come to *effect* this union, but to *declare* its existence, and to edify and console us by his life and sympathetic death. He emphasizes the "multitudinism" of their principles. The Church is not the Jewish nation or any particular sect, but the entire world, from a certain point of view, as Rigg formulates his opinion: "The Church is the world lifting itself up into the sunshine. The world is the Church falling back into shadow and darkness." Hence, too, Judaic literature has not the monopoly of the Holy Spirit. Its influence is traced in all worthy literature, poetry, romance, science, etc.; indeed, some critics declare his doctrine of the Spirit to have been Pantheistic. Kingsley remained a respected member of the Anglican ministry. He was rector of Eversley for twenty years.

In the meantime, another school of rationalizing theologians was in active operation at Oxford, and here a reaction was provoked. At Oriel there was a liberal school, headed by Whateley, Hampden, and Thomas Arnold. The latter, the famous head-master of Rugby, was one of the most strenuous defenders of Broad Church principles, and held advanced views on the inspiration of Scripture. Cambridge, at that period, was the main centre of the Low Church party. The Broad Church agreed with the Low in being anti-formal and anti-sacramentarian. Both laid the greater stress on the quality of personal conduct and inner righteousness, and detested Romanism and the Romanizing High Church as word-splitters, and as attributing a sort of magical value to external objects and ceremonies. Now, the spirit of Laud had always haunted Oxford, and it at length evoked a powerful school, headed by Froude, Pusey, Keble, and Newman. The new High Church became deeply zealous for the ritual which the Low Church neglected, and the dogmas which the Broad Church were neglecting. They began the famous Tractarian movement.

In 1833 Newman published the first "Tract for the Times," and sounded the note of war. During the next seven years ninety tracts appeared from Oriel, principally from the pens of Pusey and Newman, making a stubborn and spirited fight for the sacramental system (against the Low Churchmen), and for the support of authority and the apostolical succession (against the liberals). The sequel is well known. The Tractarians themselves fell foul of "authority." More than 150 prominent members of the movement went over to Rome. The remainder, rallying round Keble and Pusey, formed the Ritualistic movement, which has found sufficient occupation since in withstanding the allurements of Rome on the one hand, and conflicts with Low Churchmen and their own authorities on the other. The Broad Church continued its growth in peace for the next twenty years. In the year 1860 the following census of the Broad Church clergymen is drawn up—by its opponents. It does not include Ireland, nor some thousands of unimportant parishes in England :—

Broad Church	Normal type	3,100
	Exaggerated type (extreme Rationalists) ...	300
	Stagnant type	700

In 1850, out of the twenty-eight bishops and archbishops thirteen belonged to the High Church, ten to the Broad Church, and five to the Low Church. In 1860 the Broad Church was still more strongly represented on the bench.

In 1850 occurred the famous Gorham controversy, which encouraged the liberty of the liberal thinkers and much discomfited their adversaries. Its final solution is fraught with significance. The Rev. G. C. Gorham had been presented by the Lord Chancellor to the living of Brampford Speke in Devon. The Bishop of Exeter refused to institute him, on the ground that he was unsound in doctrine. He denied that regeneration is in all cases wrought by baptism. The case was brought before the Court of the Arches, the highest ecclesiastical tribunal in England, in 1849, and the Dean decided in favour of the bishop. In the following year the case was carried on to the Privy Council, of which the Queen is a member, and from which there is no appeal. The decision of the Court of the Arches was reversed, and Gorham obtained his institution. On the doctrinal point the Council said that there had always been disputes among the Reformers and among the Anglican divines; and it went on to say that the Court of the Arches had no jurisdiction to settle matters of faith, or to determine what ought, in any particular, to be the doctrine of the Church. " The duty extends only to the consideration of that which is by law established to be the doctrine of the Church of England, upon the true and legal construction of her Articles and formularies." The two archbishops acquiesced in the decision; the Bishop of London refused to do so. At the bewildering and undignified spectacle, the High Church party again fell into a panic, and numbers, including the two Wilberforces and Manning, seceded to Rome. The liberals continued a steady development.

The Broad Church had now arrived at a second and more acute stage of development, especially with regard to Scripture. The first Broad Church had made antagonism to endless punishment and to the common notion of sin one of its principal specialities; the second Broad Church principally attacks the evangelical view of Scripture—German criticism was advancing rapidly. The first Broad Church had admitted that the inspiration of Scripture differs in *kind* as well as in *degree* from that of all other books; the second school only admits difference in degree, and avows that the Bible errs wherever it contradicts science.

The leader of this school was the celebrated Master of Baliol, Dr. Jowett. In a commentary on the "Epistles to the Thessalonians, Galatians, and Romans" he expressed Rationalistic views, which were afterwards developed in "Essays and Reviews." He considered that the doctrine of atonement was involved in hopeless perplexities; that the terms "sacrifice" and "atonement" were used by the Scriptural writers in an accommodating sense, as they were familiar to the Jews; that we really know nothing of the nature of the objective act by which God reconciled the world; that Christ did not die to appease the divine wrath —the great advantage we derive from him is, not his death, but his life.

Another important member of the school, though not so overt, was Dr. Arnold's pupil and biographer, Arthur Stanley, Dean of Westminster. In his brilliant writings there is ample evidence of his liberal views on inspiration, on the accuracy of the Bible, and on miracles. He exulted warmly over the acquittal of the rationalizing writers of "Essays and Reviews," and maintained that no passage in that volume contradicted the formularies of the Church in a sense that was at all comparable to the contradiction of the articles by the High Church or of the prayer-book by the Low Church. In the *Edinburgh Review* he described with approval the wide spread of Broad Church principles. Matthew Arnold, the well-known poet and literary critic, may be mentioned as an extreme type of the Broad Church. Although a sceptic of a very advanced character—he and Carlyle are the two great representatives of what is known as "literary" Rationalism—he retained his connection with the Established Church. He was one of the most effective instruments of the diffusion of the Rationalistic spirit among the Anglican laity. "His design was," says an ecclesiastical writer, "to retain the morality of the Old and the New Testament without retaining what he thought its superstitious excrescences—miracles, the promise of a future life after death, etc."

In the second half of the century the Rationalistic movement adopts a much bolder and more candid tone of expression. There are further conflicts with ecclesiastical authority which terminate, like the Gorham controversy, in the triumph of the liberal spirit and the overruling of sacerdotal dogmatism by the State Council. The words of the Privy Council, defining and limiting the province of the ecclesiastical court, encouraged freedom of speculation on the part of professed ministers, and the Church was thrown into violent commotion by the new teaching. In the Gorham case, the Archbishops of York and Canterbury acquiesced in the final decision; in the two famous controversies which now arose the decision was evidently very unacceptable to them, and virtually deprived them of the power of checking Freethought.

The first storm arose in the year 1861. Seven prominent divines of the Broad Church united in an effort to popularize their principles, and issued, with that intention, the famous volume entitled "Essays and Reviews." In the first essay Frederick Temple, D.D., divides the period of human history into three stages—childhood, youth, and maturity. In the first stage men were ruled by precepts; in the second, guided by example; and the third stage (at which we have now arrived) is one of independent reflection and of the supremacy of conscience. He consistently extenuates the meaning of Providence and Inspiration by a universal extension; he describes the development of the world in naturalistic fashion, and says that the Hebrew type was no more divine than the Greek or Roman. In the second essay, by R. Williams, D.D., conscience is again awarded a supremacy over the Bible. The author reviews, with manifest approval, Bunsen's theories on Scripture, praises the work of the higher critics, and deplores the "literalism" of "the despairing school" (evangelical theologians). Justification by faith means simply the attainment of peace of mind by trust in a righteous God, and not a fiction of merit by transfer. Regeneration is not a reconciliation of the soul, but an awakening of its forces. In the third essay

Baden Powell, M.A., attacks miracles as being an impossible contravention of physical laws, and not in harmony with God's dealings in the natural world; all alleged miracles are the result of natural causes. The fourth essay, by H. B. Wilson, B.D., advocates the Multitudinist principle; the author urges the abrogation of all subscription to creeds and articles, so that the Church may embrace the whole nation. C. W. Goodwin, M.A., in the next essay, attacks the Scriptural cosmogony; it is found to be a purely human utterance, and is utterly falsified by modern science. Mark Patterson, B.D., in the next essay, eulogizes the Deists of the last century for their strenuous support of the supremacy of reason; the eighteenth century was the hopeful dawn of reason; now is the full noonday of its light. In the seventh essay B. Jowett returns to his theme of the interpretation of Scripture; it is the most destructive essay of the group. He finds no foundation whatever in the gospels or epistles for any supernatural view of inspiration. There is no reason for thinking that the writers of Scripture had any extraordinary gift, or were guarded from error.

Notwithstanding the advance liberalism had made, and its many earlier expressions, the "Essays and Reviews" that appeared at Oxford created a profound sensation. A fierce controversy raged throughout the Church, in which nearly four hundred publications appeared. High and Low Churchmen combined in the attack; the Church of Rome awaited patiently, with a grim smile, the issue of the mutiny. Hengstenburg, a German evangelical divine, declared it to be the "echo of German infidelity which we hear from the midst of the English Church;" that the essayists were "parrots," and that their essays "all tend towards Atheism." The Convocations of York and Canterbury fulminated against them. The High Church party sent petitions to be signed all over the country, with frantic appeals to the piety of the clergy. Nine thousand clergymen responded, and petitioned that action should be taken in the matter. In point of fact, the result only confirmed the impression of the strength of the Rationalists; as Dean Stanley triumphantly pointed out, the list only comprises one-third of the London clergy, nine professors at Oxford and one at Cambridge, eight deans (out of thirty), two headmasters of public schools, and six out of fifty clerical contributors to Smith's "Dictionary of the Bible."

However, action was taken, and Dr. Williams and Mr. Wilson were summoned before the Court of Arches. Out of thirty-two charges all were dismissed but five, and on June 21st, 1864, the Court pronounced that they had departed from the teaching of the Thirty-nine Articles on Inspiration, Atonement, and Justification. They were suspended from their functions for one year only. But the Rationalists were determined upon a severer test, and they carried an appeal before the Privy Council. Again the Privy Council reversed the decision of the ecclesiastical court, gave the essayists the costs of the case, and restored them to their functions. "On the general tendency of the book called 'Essays and Reviews,'" said the Council, "we neither can nor do pronounce an opinion. On the short extracts before us our judgment is that the charges are not proved."

In the meantime there had been another startling manifestation of the Rationalistic spirit, on this occasion in the ranks of the episcopacy itself. John William Colenso had been appointed Bishop of Natal in 1854, and sent to control the South African Mission. The natives, however, occasioned the conversion of the Bishop to Rationalism. Translating the Old Testament into Zulu brought his attention very acutely to bear upon its interesting contents, and when a Zulu one day naïvely asked him if the narrative he had been reading—the graphic description of the flood—were true, he felt a pricking of conscience in giving the orthodox answer. As the result of his studies he issued, in 1862, in the very height of the "Essays and Reviews" trouble, a book entitled "The Pentateuch and Book of Joshua Critically Examined," of which he denied the Mosaic authorship and the historical veracity, pointing out its numerous internal contradictions. The English bishops were alarmed, and all (except three) wrote a letter asking him to resign his see; and the convocations of York and Canterbury again condemned the work. Colenso refused to resign, and declared his intention of returning to Africa.

Since the English Court had no jurisdiction over him, an episcopal synod met in Cape Town on November 27th, 1863, and condemned him in his absence. He was charged with denial of the Atonement and the divinity of Christ, belief in justification without knowledge of Christ, denial of the endlessness of punishment and of the truthfulness and inspiration of Scripture. English Rationalists rallied round him, and collected £2,000 for an appeal to the Privy Council. The Council decided in favour of Colenso, and declared the sentence of the Bishop of Cape Town to be null and void. Of the religious state of South Africa after Colenso's return a bewildered Mussulman wrote to a Constantinopolitan paper: "The priests all advocate different creeds; and, as to their bishops, one Colenso actually writes books against his own religion." When Colenso revisited England in 1874, the Bishops of London, Oxford, and Lincoln forbade him to preach in their dioceses.

Thus the Broad Church advanced with rapid strides from year to year. There was no longer a necessity for the timid reserve and the veiled utterances of its early prophets. Their position was now fully recognised in the Church, and their speculations were practically unassailable, except by argument. They assimilated the results of modern thought with surprising facility, in the departments of higher criticism, philosophy, and science; and they continued to develop the ethical modifications of dogma of their predecessors. Indeed, now that Jowett's "Life and Letters" have been given to the world, his Rationalism is found to have been most destructive. One reviewer says of him: "He regarded them [the creeds] as extinct superstitions...... He scarcely believed in a personal Deity, and less and less as life went on......He rejected miracles entirely, the Resurrection, of course, included......of the doctrine of the pardon of sins he had no conception." Mr. Mallock has happily delineated his position in "The New Republic." Dr. Jenkinson (Jowett) preaches the Sunday sermon in the private theatre, whereupon the opinion of the Agnostic professor (Huxley) is given that, apart from unavoidable matters of form, he finds himself in substantial agreement with the divine. The incident is typical of the attitude of a large section of Churchmen.

In the year after the decision on "Essays and Reviews" an important legislative measure was introduced for the express purpose of strengthening the position of the Broad Churchmen. The terms of subscription to the Thirty-nine

Articles had now become a matter of grave concern to clerical aspirants with modern views of dogma and ritual and Scripture. The High Church party, though equally distant from their letter, subscribed to them with that easy elasticity of conscience which invariably comes of contact with Rome; but many of the Rationalists were much disturbed by a form of subscription which demanded an "unfeigned assent and consent to all and everything contained in the book of Common Prayer." Dean Stanley once more came to the front, and had a correspondence with Archbishop Tait on the subject. "If once," he wrote, "we press the subscriptions in their rigid and literal sense, it may safely be asserted that there is not one clergyman in the Church who can venture to cast a stone at another; they must all go out." The statement was only too evidently true, and in 1865 Lord Granville introduced a Bill in which the form of subscription was materially altered. Instead of giving an "unfeigned assent to all and everything" in the articles and book of prayer, the clergyman merely professed: "I believe the doctrine of the Church of England, as therein set forth, to be agreeable to the word of God." By accepting the doctrine (in the singular number) they were dispensed from assenting to individual dogmas, and they had no difficulty in considering that doctrine, of whose moral character they were deeply convinced, to be "agreeable to the word of God" (as expounded and expurged by the higher critics). The change has a very deep significance, and is one of the most tangible of the many signs of the times which permit us to test the strength of the Rationalistic current. As Buxton said, in the House of Commons, the Bill was introduced "to make it possible for men to minister at the altars of the church, though they might dissent from some part of her teaching." The Bill passed into law, 28 and 29 Vict., c. 122.

There is an interesting passage in one of Stanley's own works which illustrates the curious obstinacy of the Rationalists in adhering to the Established Church. "The choice," he says, in his "Essays on Church and State," "is between absolute individual separation from every conceivable outward form of organization and continuance in one or other of those which exist in the hope of modifying or improving it.......The path of a theologian or ecclesiastic who, in any existing system, loves truth and seeks charity is, indeed, difficult at the best......To serve a great institution, and by serving it to endeavour to promote within it a vitality which shall secure it as the shelter for such as will have to continue the same struggle after they are gone, is an object for which much may be, and ought to be, endured, which otherwise would be intolerable." He conceived the national church to be, not a rigid and unchanging institution, but a body whose function it was to promulgate the truths which approve themselves *in each successive generation*, and as the most efficient instrument for supplying the moral needs of the community. And that was the attitude of all the rationalizing divines. They looked to the ethical and philanthropic value of Christianity, and the theistic basis of its altruistic spirit, as they conceived it; to the fate of its dogmas and formulæ they were comparatively indifferent. They could thus assimilate freely the results of destructive criticism; it might reveal other religious systems of equal ethical value, but it could never impair the inherent value of Christianity. And the Church of England was useful as a barrier to Roman and ritualistic tyranny. How that frame of mind is related to the modern ethical movement will appear in chapter v.

During the next thirty years the growth of the movement is constant and devoid of dramatic interest. England has become accustomed to liberal concessions on the part of its ministers. At the present day they are both frequent and generous, yet they excite little or no official protest, and little excitement outside the pages of third-rate periodicals. The supremacy of conscience and the freedom of individual speculation, contained in germ in the fundamental principle of the Reformation, is now virtually accepted. Ecclesiastical authority is practically limited to administrative functions. From the recognition that the Church had no supernatural commission in teaching men quickly came to recognise that the time-honoured ecclesiastical formularies were equally devoid of supernatural sanction, and are at length learning to extend the same view to the Judaic literature on which they were founded. The magisterial power of prelates has grown more attenuated with each succeeding decade: the Lincoln case was another illustration of its fictitious ascendancy. Clergymen speculate freely in complete disregard both of prelates and formularies, and their opinions almost cover the entire ground between Romanism and Agnosticism. I know one who considers the Archbishop of Westminster as his lawful prelate; and, at the other extreme, the pupils of Jowett, with their neo-Platonic divinity, are not far removed from Agnosticism. When Canon Farrar, preaching in Westminster Abbey, rejected one of the most characteristic dogmas of Christianity there was a momentary excitement; but it has long subsided into indifference. And when, in 1889, Canon Gore edited "Lux Mundi," which started from the assumption that, in this epoch of "profound transformation," theology "must take a new development," and that there was a "necessity of some general restatement of the claims and meanings of theology," a few of the more fossilized theologians, like Archdeacon Denison, raised a solemn protest; but the book was only another welcome expression of a very wide-spread sentiment. Men like Professor Momerie can with impunity preach, in pulpits of the Established Church, rank disbelief in the most familiar dogmas. Other clergymen, like A. Craufurd, M.A., in his "Christian Instincts and Modern Doubt," propagate by their writings a similar rejection of all dogma (in the traditional sense), and a commendation of the spirit of Emerson and Browning. Even, to judge from the posthumous revelations on the late Archbishop of York, the Rationalistic spirit is not confined to the minor spheres.

It would be impossible to appreciate the working of the Rationalistic spirit among the laity of the Church of England, for the simple reason that one does not know where to draw the line of communion. If Mr. Matthew Arnold, with his professed abhorrence of all dogma and his shadowy remnant of theistic belief, is aggregated to it, its comprehension is bewildering. The author of "Supernatural Religion," a book which caused a fluttering of wings in 1874, is just as anti-miraculous as Mr. Arnold. Sir J. Seeley, another prominent lay writer, author of "Ecce Homo," is also conspicuously Rationalistic. Few Rationalists (retaining some shade of Theistic belief) have placed themselves outside the pale of the Church as decisively as Carlyle did; yet Carlyle was more decidedly Theistic than Arnold. Drummond, Balfour, and Mallock, the three chief modern champions of the Church, are decided Rationalists; the latter two decided sceptics. Of the poets who have influenced the nineteenth century, Wordsworth, Southey, Coleridge, Shelley, Byron, Keats, Browning, Tennyson, G. Eliot, A. Clough, Swinburne, Arnold—how few can honestly be said to have remained in the Church? The list is a perfect gradation of stages of the Rationalistic spirit—from Wordsworth to Shelley. We can only say that, on perusing a list of the secular writers of the century, especially of the present day, in poetry, fiction, history, science, ethics, and philosophy, the majority are found to be at least anti-dogmatic and anti-sacerdotal, and to take no more than a moral interest in the Established Church.

Such, then, has been the evolution of the Rationalistic spirit in the Church itself since the beginning of the century. The century opens with the apparent triumph of theologians over the Deistic school, the last embodiment of Rationalistic inquiry. A storm of vituperation greets the appearance of "The Age of Reason." By the middle of the century a book, virtually containing the same principles, is published by a group of professed theologians at Oxford, acclaimed by half the nation, and sanctioned by the highest tribunal of the land. The end of the century is in a fair way to accept even the conclusions of Paine on dogma and Scripture. A similar progress is seen in every other land that is freed from the ignorance and sacerdotal tyranny of the past; but the limits of this sketch confine our attention to England. Germany, Switzerland, France, Holland, and the United States can boast a similar history. Now, however, for the clearer analysis of that progress which has been historically described, we have to consider the particular dogmas of traditional theology which have been modified or rejected, and the influences which effected that remarkable expansion.

One of the most potent influences at work in the direction of Rationalism has been the system of Biblical criticism which has attained such curious results and adopted so subversive a tone in the present century. This will demand special treatment in the next chapter. A third chapter will estimate the important effect of recent discoveries in comparative religion; and the influence of science and philosophy will be separately considered. At present we are concerned with an influence which is not a result of the recent accumulation of knowledge, and so not peculiar to this century, except in the intensity of its operation—it is the action of reason in itself, apart from its recent attainments, upon dogma. This is the most natural element of the Rationalistic spirit, and it is this direct application of reason to dogma, initiated by the Kantist-Coleridgean school, and consistently maintained by all the Broad Churchmen, which has had so dissolving an effect upon the old beliefs. As Kant first clearly associated and differentiated the speculative and the practical functions of reason, so there has been a twofold application of it in the present instance. Some dogmas have fallen before conscience proper, the moral sense; some have yielded to purely speculative considerations.

Among the doctrines which have dissolved under candid and sincere ethical consideration, the most familiar is that of the eternity of punishment. With a larger development of the moral sense and the attainment of a certain degree of liberty of thought, it was inevitable that this, the most repellent point of the Christian scheme, should be toned down. No admixture of Kantist or Platonist speculation was necessary for its modification. The emancipated moral sense at once perceived and declared its incompatibility with the high attributes which were assigned to the Deity. Hence the dogma was an object of adverse criticism from the very beginning of liberal speculation. The decisions of the Privy Council in '64 made it clear that the teaching of the Thirty-nine Articles on the point could be set aside with impunity. Canon Farrar in 1877 placidly remarked of the decaying doctrine: "Many of us were scared with it in our childhood;" and Frothingham says that it has not only departed from the temples of science and philosophy, but " even in the wilderness of theology it is seldom met with."

Lecky has analyzed the immoral effect the doctrine is calculated to have upon those who subscribe to it: (1) It causes an indifference to suffering, for the habitual contemplation of such scenes of horror as Christian ministers formerly depicted to their audiences could not but blunt the edge of sensitiveness. (2) It stifles the natural feeling of pity for suffering; the believer is constrained to regard this picture of inhuman torment as the deliberate infliction of his Deity; indeed, he is taught that such will be his mental condition in the abode of bliss that he will look down with complacency on the fearful fate of his dearest friends. (3) It predisposes to persecution; the terrible example of the divine chastiser sanctions the minor terrestrial persecutions of the Inquisition, and of every period and section of Christianity.

On the other hand, the efforts of rationalizing theologians to explain away the pellucid teaching of Christ on the subject are painfully ingenious. Maurice drew a distinction between eternal and everlasting which is difficult to less subtle minds. H. Ward-Beecher says: "I doubt whether in the days of the Old Testament, or in the Jewish mind at the time of our Saviour, the sharp, metaphysically-accurate idea of time and duration existed. I believe that what they meant by eternal was a vague and nebulous period of time, and that it was not used in a scientific sense, but in a poetic." When Canon Farrar preached his famous five sermons on the subject in Westminster Abbey, he said, after describing the traditional belief: "Though texts may be quoted which give *primâ facie* plausibility to such modes of teaching, yet, to say nothing of the fact that the light and love which God himself has kindled within us recoil from them, these texts are, in the first place, alien to the broad, unifying principles of Scripture. That, in the next place, they are founded on interpretations demonstrably groundless; and, in the third place, that for every one so quoted two can be adduced to the contrary." And he concludes: "Thus, then, finding neither in Scripture nor anywhere anything to prove that the fate of every man is at death irrevocably determined, I shake off the hideous incubus of atrocious conceptions attached by false theology to the doctrine of final retribution." With such words, spoken by the first preacher in the first temple of the English Church, the "hideous incubus" may be dismissed for ever.

So universal and emphatic is the rejection of this treasured doctrine of nineteen centuries of Christendom that antipathy to it has actually penetrated into the Church of Rome—so aptly compared by Dr. Jessopp to the Celestial Empire. In the *Irish Ecclesiastical Record* there had appeared an article extenuating the harsh features of the dogma, and teaching that one might lawfully hope that the damned came at length to a state of "something like submissive contentment." A similarly timid article followed in the *Dublin Review*. At length, in 1892, Professor Mivart commenced a series of articles on the question in the *Nineteenth Century*. He had frequently voiced what little liberal sentiment there was in the Church of Rome. Cardinal Newman had, in his "Grammar of Assent," revived (from Petavius) an ancient notion that the damned were granted an alleviation of their sufferings from time to time. But Mivart thought it consistent with Papal doctrine to admit, not only that the damned find a certain complacency in the society of kindred souls, but even that there may be an evolution or amelioration of their sufferings in the course of time. He did not reject the word "fire,' but he naïvely added that "the Church does not mean by fire anything like what we do." Dr. Mivart thought that the whispers of the time-spirit were as audible in the Church of Rome as elsewhere. "This reaction," he says, "I rejoice to help forward, for I am sure that the hour has fully come for putting away such revolting images." Rome thought otherwise, and the articles were put on the Index. Such condemnation, however, is regarded only as a matter of discipline by educated Catholics, and commands only external compliance. In point of fact, many Catholics still retain Mr. Mivart's half-hearted theory.

Another point of traditional doctrine to which the early Broad Church, according to Hurst, offered an equal resistance is the idea of sin. Gunsaulus, an American critic of much competency, says that "Coleridge and his followers have so infringed upon the fundamental idea that their idea of sin is......possible only in Pantheism." Jowett's idea of sin has frequently been said to be Pantheistic. Gunsaulus says of him that "he buries his orthodoxy, with all the ideas of sin and a personal God it has cherished, in his essay on 'Predestination and Free-will.'"* As we have seen previously, they all agreed that sin was not a matter of guilt or of responsibility, not a positive consequence of transgression of a divine law. Its character was "negative" and "unreal," it was merely a regrettable condition of life.

* "The Metamorphoses of a Creed," by F. W. Gunsaulus.

Indeed, Maurice gives somewhere a fantastic description of sin as consisting in the fact that some men (the good) recognise their redemption in Christ, and others (the sinful) do not; all, however, were redeemed once for all by Christ; and he says, in a letter to Miss Barton, that he "wishes to treat evil as though it were not, for in very truth it is a falsehood." In point of fact, the Rationalizers were approaching that saner view of the moral law which Bentham initiated, and which is now current among us—that, namely, which ascribes the character of a humanitarian ordination to the moral law, and does not base it upon the arbitrary will of a Supreme Being. On that theory each sin leaves its inevitable imprint in human life, for which there is no atonement. At the same time men were beginning to recognise that the theory of the divine chastiser was an imperfectly sublimated relic of pre-civilized ages. Anger and vindictiveness were coming to be recognised as unseemly attributes of the Platonic deity of the nineteenth century.

And this conception of sin was applied with even greater eagerness to the traditional dogma of original sin. As the moral sense of the community asserted its supreme position it came to throw off that plea of "mystery" which had confusedly reconciled Christendom to so grave an ethical anomaly as the condemnation of countless millions of men to positive, even eternal, suffering for one man's fault. In proportion as the moral sense is refined in man, it recedes with abhorrence from that course of conduct which tradition had assigned to an infinitely good and moral being. During so many centuries conscience had been stifled by the plea of mystery; but conscience triumphed at last and rejected the imputed conduct. It is only from Roman Catholic quarters that we now hear such words as these: "It is a heresy to *deny* that the souls of unbaptized babies are guilty of sin, or that they are punished for their guilt."* Many of the Broad Churchmen began to hope for a change in the baptismal service (though the Gorham case had reduced it purely to a matter of form). Maurice wished that, instead of presuming to *make* the infant a child of God, it would simply *declare* it to be one.

* The Bishop of Nottingham in a pastoral against Mivart.

But the great struggle of the century between the Broad Church and the orthodox, and one which is closely connected with the theory of sin, is over the question of the Atonement. If sin is not a matter of guilt and responsibility, and if vindictive punishment is thought unworthy of the Deity, then the traditional conception of the Atonement must be discarded. Hence the liberals at once began to change entirely the character of the dogma. God is represented in the new school as a principle of infinite love; his whole dispensation is marked with love, not with anger and vindictiveness, as a less enlightened religious feeling conceived it to be. Hence there is nothing to be seen in the Atonement but love; the cruder elements of "punishment" and "victim of divine wrath," etc., must be relegated to the ages that imported them into the Biblical conception. Coleridge protests against the notion that Christ paid a debt for us; sin does not incur a debt. Trench says that the Atonement was quite independent of the Fall of Adam. Maurice and Kingsley protest against its being considered as a reconciliation of a sinful humanity and an angry Deity. Jowett's refined moral sense declares that sacrifice is a "crude and barbarous notion"—a relic of the ancient days when savages thought their gods eat and drank like themselves—and that there is no sacrificial idea in the Atonement. Only in a figurative sense can we speak of the "sacrifice of the cross"—the phrase which has been on the lips of Christendom for nineteen centuries. J. Macleod Campbell, of the Scotch Established Church, says it was "a moral and spiritual atonement;" justice looks to the sinner, not as an object of punishment, but simply as being in the undesirable condition of unrighteousness. In a word, the whole of the Rationalizers, like the schools of Schleiermacher and Hofmann in Germany, and the corresponding school in the United States, reject the familiar Christian doctrine that Christ procured salvation for humanity. That is a step of profound significance.

Still they retain, as usually happens, most of the old terminology, though the sense of the word has entirely changed. Setting aside such as deny the divinity of Christ, they have several theories of the death of the Son of God. Some look upon it as a sensible representation to humanity of the enormity of sin; the majority, however, make it a direct part of their scheme of universal divine love. Humanity, they say, was never really separated from God, as the old theology taught; we are not born children of wrath, etc., but all in all times are embraced in the divine love. But a striking revelation of that union became necessary, hence the economy of the Atonement, which was, says Jowett, "the greatest moral act ever done in the world," and "God's method of conquering the human heart, and subduing a revolted world, and attaching it to his throne." Hence, too, the death of Christ was only the dramatic termination of the episode, not the unique source of merit. It is through Christ's exemplary *life* we are most benefitted. Whatever may be thought of the ethical value of this new dogma, its substitution for the old one is revolutionary to the Christian scheme.

Besides the more obvious consequences of the new method of conceiving Christ's mission, it was soon perceived that it removed one of the gravest reasons for believing in his divinity. The old argument was that no finite atonement could efface the infinite indignity of sin, hence it was necessary for man's salvation that a divine being should atone for him. Now that there was no infinite debt to repay, and that the notion of vicarious atonement was rejected by the purified theology, why should Christ be divine at all? For the supposed purpose of the "atonement" (as they persisted in calling it) the sacrifice of a Buddha or a Socrates would suffice. In the answer of the orthodox theologians there is much confusion and inadequacy. It is said no one of them would admit that he denied the divinity of Christ (though Jowett and Colenso are accused of doing so); but their replies are very unsatisfactory. They generally say that this dramatic representation of the evil of sin and of the love of God was to be an "overwhelming spectacle," and evoke a "tremendous sympathy;" and thus they infer the divinity of the victim from the strength of their adjectives. Still, they have been watched with much anxiety on the point, and a denial of Christ's divinity is feared as a further development.

When Canon Gore edited "Lux Mundi" his criticism of Christ's references to the Old Testament was felt by many to be dangerous. He, however, resists the interpretation. Only Momerie, Craufurd, and a few minor Rationalists are explicit on the point.* In "Ecce Homo" Sir J. Seeley did not openly call into question the divinity of Christ, but the eagerness with which he emphasizes the natural beauty and elevation of his character is very suggestive.

Another doctrine which had been particularly prominent since the Reformation, and which has now been rejected by the majority of thoughtful believers, is the supposed meritoriousness of faith. "Only believe and you shall be saved" was not merely an ironical summary of Protestant doctrine; it was a very widely-accepted principle. Now, however, it has yielded to the strong infusion of ethical consideration which characterizes modern religious thought. The value of a man's life is measured almost entirely by his works. The confusion which has long enveloped the meaning of faith has been largely removed, and it is very commonly regarded, not as an arbitrary preternatural gift of mysterious nature, nor as a vague sentiment overriding the workings of reason, but as an intellectual assent like any other, only to be accorded on the perception of satisfactory evidence. The acceptance of definite creeds and formularies is understood to be a matter of secondary importance; the true test of communion with the Church of Christ is righteousness of life. And there has been a profound change, also, in the conception of the works which prove genuine moral worth. The older ascetical idea has fallen into disrepute. The anger of God has disappeared from the circle of religious thought; "the religion of Christ," says Momerie, in this connection, "has no angry Deity requiring to be bribed." Love is now, in the modern Johannine Church, his most prominent attribute; hence it must be thought that he surrounded human life with pleasures, not for purposes of mortification, but for the enjoyment of his children. Works that yield fruit of human happiness or of evil undone are the only acceptable gifts; the selfish, timorous, and useless asceticism of former days is relegated to the gallery of religious pathology. Kingsley ridicules it in his brilliant novels; Tennyson indicates its futility in impressive verse; Jowett thinks sacrifice to the Infinite a barbaric notion.

* Momerie says, in "Defects of Christianity," that the character of Christ is "so different from those of ordinary men as to deserve and demand that we should call it, by way of contradistinction, divine."

And simultaneously with this cessation of belief in the merit of faith there has spread a refusal to admit the demerit of unbelief as such. This attitude is more particularly a result of nineteenth-century evolution, for the Reformers were as ready to burn the unbeliever as their predecessors. With the multiplication of sects a more lenient view of theological error was inevitable, and even Chillingworth admitted "the absolute innocence of error." Yet this leniency was only extended to the absolute unbeliever with much unwillingness, and under a kind of moral compulsion. We have seen how, in the early years of this century, even the Deism of Paine was grievously persecuted; and even the illustrious De Maistre believed that infidels always died of horrible diseases with special names. Truth, however, has prevailed; in face of the glorious list of "unbelieving" Englishmen of the nineteenth century—a veritable legion of honour —quoted in the Introduction, no one who has not had the perverse training of a Roman Catholic, or who does not live in the emotional atmosphere of the lower Evangelical school, can sustain the "pestilent doctrine" of the sinfulness of scepticism. Yet the doctrine is still embodied in the formularies of the Anglican Church. As Stanley pointed out to Archbishop Tait, according to the Athanasian creed (contained in the Prayer-book to which the clergyman subscribes) all the Greeks are hopelessly damned, since they do not admit that the Holy Ghost proceeds from the Father *and* the Son; yet he quotes, with warm approval, the words of a "great prelate": "I never met with a single clergyman who believed this in the literal sense of the words." Again, the 18th article runs: "They also are to be had accursed that presume to say that every man shall be saved by the Law or Sect which he professeth, so that he be diligent to frame his life according to that Law and the light of nature. For Holy Scripture doth set out unto us only the name of Jesus Christ, whereby men must be saved."

With this compare the following words from one of the Rev. A. Momerie's sermons: "Many so-called infidels and atheists are among the most zealous servants of God." And even bishops have endorsed that panegyric of the avowed "infidel"—Charles Darwin. However, this question will recur in the last chapter.

The doctrine of Predestination has also been profoundly

modified by the ethical spirit of the Rationalists. The Lutheran doctrine was, of course, less repulsive (in direct form) than the Calvinistic from the commencement; yet it was repulsive enough, and the believer was once more urged to distort his conscience into accepting it as a profound and painful mystery. The modern conscience has solved the mystery, to some extent, by refusing to believe in the predestination of a few chosen souls—and the inevitable damnation of the majority. Kingsley, Temple, Wilson, and Colenso strenuously urged a more generous estimate of the fate of humanity and of the extension of the Church; they declare the older view—the belief of nineteen centuries—to be a blasphemy. H. Ward Beecher says it would drive him to infidelity. The working of Providence has been recognised in other religions besides Judaism and Christianity, and discovered on earth in the tens of thousands of years that preceded the death of Christ; the gift of Inspiration has been accorded to other literatures than the Hebrew and the Hebræo-Greek.

Finally, the activity of that important figure in Christian theology—the devil—has been considerably restricted, not only by scientific, but by ethical considerations. During the long history of Christianity its adherents looked with unmoved complacency on the spectacle of endless legions of devils let loose among mankind to tempt, afflict, corrupt, ruin in body and soul the less gifted children of Adam : the Irish peasant regards that view to this day as a divine revelation, and accepts it just as calmly as the belief that nearly the whole of humanity will be condemned to indescribable torment for not embracing his own peculiar tenets. Science initiated a revolt by exposing the cruel fallacy of witchcraft and superseding exorcisms; as it advances "Satan retreats," says Frothingham, "from one department of nature after another, and leaves the highways and byways of creation free to the passage of serene, inexorable, and regenerating law." And at length the ethical enormity of the old belief dawns upon the Christian conscience. Various efforts are made to explain away Christ's continual references to devils ; indeed, one modern theologian maintains that the obnoxious idea comes rather from Milton's "Paradise Lost" than from the Bible. In any case, the modern moralist traces evil to more tangible influences, and pays less regard to the powers of darkness. The wide acceptance of a modern work of fiction in which Satan's character is completely revolutionized must be taken as a symptom of the decay of the dogma.

Of the points of doctrine which have suffered from criticism of a purely intellectual nature the most conspicuous is the belief in miracles. Christendom seems to have been a perpetual theatre of miraculous events until the Reformation, when they suddenly cease, and faith looks back for their occurrence to the early ages of the Church and to Scripture. Early in the century the patristic miracles are disregarded, and attention confined to those enumerated in Scripture. As the Rationalistic spirit gains strength it boldly attacks the miracles of Scripture; for, says Mr. Lecky, "the first work of Rationalism is an attempt to explain away the miracles of Scripture." Julius Hare, with a presentiment of the fatal results of German criticism, prepares the attack by teaching that too much importance had been attached to the Scripture miracles; the real and enduring basis of Christianity is its fulfilment of the moral necessities of mankind—miracles are a superfluous adornment of its structure. Baden Powell, in "Essays and Reviews," makes a direct attack upon the very abstract idea of a miracle. Stanley also is liberal on the point. The author of "Supernatural Religion," in 1874, takes as his formal object the task of proving that the miraculous element in Christianity is a delusion. He maintains (1) that miracles are not only highly improbable, but antecedently incredible, so that no amount of testimony would avail, as Hume held and Voltaire denied; and (2) that the actual witnesses to the New Testament miracles, the writers of the Gospels and Epistles, are not entitled to credence. Matthew Arnold is conspicuously anti-miraculous. On the whole, the objection, or at least indifference, to them which is now so common arises, not so much from a belief in their intrinsic impossibility (as the Deists held), or the fallibility of testimony (as Hume held), as from the fact, so clearly enunciated by Huxley, that we are absolutely ignorant of the capabilities of "nature," and therefore illogical in introducing supernatural forces to explain phenomena. Among miracles, of course, the resurrection of the body must be included, and there has been a decay of belief in that scriptural doctrine.

Hurst* declares that Maurice did not accept it in the orthodox sense. Momerie maintains that Scripture does not promise a resurrection of the material body at all.

The dogma of the Trinity has invited Rationalistic criticism from the time of its formation—the fourth century. Since, however, the dogma has become the fundamental tenet of the orthodox Church, in contradistinction to Arians, Socinians, or Unitarians, few important ecclesiastics openly dissent from it. Kingsley's doctrine of the holy spirit is said to have been Pantheistic. Jowett and Colenso are generally said to have abandoned it. The Rev. A. Craufurd and the Rev. A. Momerie openly reject it. Momerie again says that Scripture never taught it; that it merely depicts the one indivisible God as manifesting himself in three characters—in nature, in Christ, and in our hearts. Thus the divinity of Christ is also called into question with impunity. In fact, there has recently been an attempt made to show that the ordinary doctrine of the Incarnation, the miraculous conception of Christ, is inconsistent with the idea that the relations of the sexes are divinely appointed. A deviation from the ordinary sexual course, in view of the sanctity of Christ, would seem to imply that there is something unholy in legitimate sexual intercourse.

Two of the most vivid convictions of the Christian from the earliest Christian ages have been belief in the personality of God and the personality of the devil. The latter, we have seen, is much enfeebled; the former has also been deeply impaired by the criticism of professed theologians. Dr. Arnold seems to have felt that a relaxation of this dogma (certainly the most important in theology) was imminent. Maurice quotes a saying of his, "that the early Church was utterly wrong and foolish in making the nature of God the ground of its belief and profession; whereas some doctrine directly concerning our human life ought to be the uniting bond." A little later Jowett wrote, with characteristic nonchalance, that "the received reasons for believing in a God are groundless." We have already quoted two critics (both ecclesiastical writers) who declare that Jowett lost belief in the personality of God. Dean Mansel also provoked strong accusation of rationalizing the dogma in his

---

* "History of Rationalism."

Bampton Lectures. He said that "a finite mind can form no conception of an infinite being which shall be speculatively true;" our knowledge of God, as the absolute and unconditioned, as he wished him to be called, is negative and regulative, not positive and speculative. Chretien says of him that he "consigns us for the guidance of our life to seeming truths, but tells us that, if we could only lay aside the veil of our human nature, we should perceive these seeming truths to be falsehoods." And even Maurice accuses him of denying that we can know God. The point will be further discussed in the chapter on philosophy.

With such specimens of the criticisms of prominent and influential theologians on the most important Christian dogmas we may fitly close our appreciation of the rationalizing tendency within the Church. Not only has there been a remarkable number of secessions from orthodoxy to Rationalism proper in the course of the century, but a large section of the Church itself is moving bodily towards that goal. In the stress of an overpowering controversy, and in the painful foreboding of its issue, there has been a deliberate and successful attempt to free the Church from the fatal shackles of dogma, and to base its fortune upon its ethical and humanitarian mission. How far, in historical retrospect, such a profound change casts discredit upon its claims as an institution it is not our province to consider; and it would be premature to essay a prediction of the probable consequences. The position will be more clearly understood after treating of Rationalism in ethics.

As an epilogue it is interesting to note the progress of the Rationalistic spirit in a sect which has hitherto preserved its clear characteristic features through eighteen centuries of troubled life. In an interesting article in the *Fortnightly Review* Mr. Cohen points out that Jewish obduracy has all but vanished, through contact with modern Rationalism. "The past half-century," he writes, "has undeniably been an epoch in Freethought, and the expanding Hebrew has exhausted the possibilities." Rabbinism is slowly dying; Judaism to-day is a species of materialism. "Homogeneity is gone, and the new order is a peaceful conglomeration of multifarious points of view." The absence of spiritualism is inferred from the unpopularity of private prayer. The

Anglo-Jewish Association entertains Mr. Bradlaugh at dinner; the number of mixed marriages increases; a sort of Jewish Young Men's Association starts with a positive doctrine of sin; it fails. A layman of some standing recommends uncovered heads at divine service and the Sabbath on the Lord's day—no one is moved. At the School Board election the preponderance of educated Jewish opinion was towards purely secular teaching in Board schools. Here, too, therefore, the Rationalistic spirit has penetrated, and has apparently triumphed in proportion to the tyranny it has undermined.

Chapter II.

BIBLICAL CRITICISM.

SIMULTANEOUSLY with the decay of formulæ and dogmata, which has been described in the preceding chapter, there has been in progress during the century a remarkable and profound change in the conception of that literature from which they are believed to have issued. The very term "Biblical criticism" is, of itself, suggestive of an important change of attitude on the part of the Christian mind. It is now one of the most familiar phrases on the lips of the modern educated world, orthodox and heterodox; yet it implies an entirely new mode of conceiving the sacred literature of Judaism and Christianity. Indeed, there is no province of thought in which the active Rationalistic spirit of this century has effected a stranger and more significant revolution than in its criticism of the Bible. The mists of ages of superstitious reverence have been marvellously dissipated. The sacred character of the book has gradually faded until—with regard to the Old Testament at least—it has entirely lost any special and distinctive features raising it to a position of authority among the sacred books of other religions; its historical value has been almost entirely destroyed, and its ethical character has been most gravely impeached. The Old Testament, in particular, has been almost rejected by the modern theologian, and, strange to say, has acquired an interest and value in the eyes of his Rationalistic adversary. In the eyes of all educated men it has now only a *similar* value—in whatever *degree* that may be estimated—to that of all other sacred books—an ethical value. The glamour of inspiration, in the specific sense understood by all previous Christianity, has departed from it for ever. It has no different inspiration than that of the Vedas, or the Zend Avesta, or the Iliad, or the Æneid, or "Paradise Lost."

Such a transformation of the conception of the Bible, even, to a large extent, of the *orthodox* conception, is an important aspect of nineteenth-century progress. Like all other branches of progress, it has its roots in the past centuries; but one hundred years ago there were still but feeble and spasmodic protests against the oppressive tyranny of the traditional view. Lessing and Semler could not have formed a remote conception of the issue of the movement, which they saw and calmly blessed before they died. Even Eichhorn and Geddes could not, in the least, have anticipated its utterly revolutionary result. But the critical attitude which they adopted and recommended harmonized too well with the mental unrest, the audacity, and the destructiveness of the new-born century. Criticism became a science of engrossing interest and of powerful effect, and ecclesiastical authority and the voice of tradition were enfeebled before the multitude of issues which the new generation raised. Like every anti-traditional effort, it was concentrated, fired, and purified by a continued stress of sacerdotal opposition; but it has at length attained so high a degree of security and cogency that it now numbers a large body of the most competent orthodox scholars among its most advanced adherents.

Some of the defects of the books of the Old Testament are so conspicuous that they had been derisively pointed out by the few Freethinkers who arose in preceding centuries; but the traditional reverence for the Bible was still too strong to permit a candid and sensible appreciation of them. The strained explanations of fathers and schoolmen were still available. There had, it is true, already been a significant change in the popular estimate of the book. The belief in verbal inspiration had practically vanished, and the painfully obvious human element had at length dawned upon the mind of Christendom. The inspiration, however, which was universally attributed to the Bible, was still of a character to repel scientific analysis, and even forbid a common-sense appreciation of its contents. Its contradictions, repetitions, impossibilities, and indecencies were still gravely attributed to the Holy Spirit, and, therefore, placed beyond criticism. Another advance towards criticism was made in the seventeenth century by the discovery of the unsatisfactory condition of the actual text of Scripture.

Until the seventeenth century divines had assumed that Providence had miraculously guarded its inspired books. From this torpid belief they were at length roused by the controversies on the date and origin of the vowel points of the Hebrew text between the Buxtorfs and Morinus and Cappell, and by the discovery of a vast number of variations in the manuscripts and printed books of Scripture—Kennicott's Hebrew Bible, published from 1776 to 1790, gave 200,000 variations. Thus a door was opened to a certain reverent kind of criticism. Here and there, as in the case of R. Simon and Leclerc, criticism assumed a more threatening character, but it was easily suppressed, and only such radical Freethinkers as Hobbes and Spinoza ventured to anticipate, in some measure, the destructive views of subsequent ages.

The eighteenth century witnessed a graver and more systematic attack upon the cherished idol. The English Deists, the German Illuminati, and the French *philosophes* made a direct attack, before the middle of the century, upon the supernatural origin of the Scriptures. Their criticism, however, was comparatively superficial, and confined itself to the obvious contradictions and gross indecencies of the narrative. It was effectually (however illogically) restrained by the theological ingenuities of excuse and conciliation which it evoked. In its old form, it perished before the end of the century. However, it had achieved an important work; it had emancipated reason and conscience, and planted the seeds of a new force, more fatal to traditional belief, and more useful to intellectual progress. The "Higher Criticism" which thus virtually commenced in the last century had an entirely different character from the Voltairean Scepticism—not an *opposite* character, but a more profound and scientific method. It is foolish to contrast nineteenth-century criticism with the older method and endeavour to make capital of their divergence. The new method recognises the destructive inferences to be drawn from the contradictions, etc., which are obvious in all versions of the Bible; but it has forged new and more powerful instruments—not only weapons of destruction, but useful implements of construction. It relies upon an accurate and profound science of philology, which finds important critical considerations in the original text of scripture—in differences of style and lexicology, and other linguistic features ; it compares the information acquired by history and archæology ;* it enters, by an intimate acquaintance with the Hebrew text, into the peculiarities of thought, the psychological conditions, as well as the material environment, of the writers. The results of the present day have been attained by the application of such methods by an unbroken series of erudite Hebraists and profound thinkers from Eichhorn to Wellhausen. Though this sketch is intended only to summarize Rationalistic progress in England, it is absolutely necessary, in this section, to treat of the German schools, in which the progress in Biblical analysis has been mainly achieved.

It is often foolishly objected to the higher criticism by English hearers that it comes from Germany. Apart from the obvious frivolity of the objection (for, whatever may be said of the German systems which come here when they die, the living thoughts of that erudite and energetic nation are of great importance to us), it may be safely answered that German criticism may be traced to an English source. In 1774-8 a number of treatises by Reimarns propagated the ideas of the English Deists throughout Germany ; these works, commonly called the "Wolfenbüttel Fragments," had a profound disturbing influence on the younger generation, though even their editor, Lessing, did not approve of the opinions they embodied. That they had an important influence, and thus directly prepared the way for the nascent "higher" criticism, is admitted by such writers as Lechler, Ritschl, Tholuck, and Dorner. Thus the present advanced stage of Biblical criticism in England may be traced back, through the activity in the German schools, to the Deistic teaching of the last century—to which it is so often unwisely opposed in a deprecatory sense. In Germany the seed had more favourable conditions for growth. The tyranny of the

---

* Though there is much confusion in contrasting the terms "higher" and "lower" criticism, it is certainly not correct to say that the "higher" criticism is purely internal and philological. In spite of Professor Sayce's assertions, the higher critics *do* utilize the results of careful research in Assyriology and Egyptology. The "lower" criticism would seem to be a purely mechanical textual criticism, such as Bengel and Wetstein initiated, and Hug, Griesbach, Scholz, Tischendorf, etc., continue.

sterner Lutheran and Calvinistic formulæ provoked a fiercer reaction, and the liberty of University Professors was in happy contrast to the demoralizing restraint of their British contemporaries. The spread of the Kantist philosophy, which discarded all but the ethical elements of religion, was also most favourable to the growth of criticism.

Under such conditions Johann Salomo Semler (1725-91), who is called the "father of modern Biblical criticism," commenced the work of disintegration. He was an orthodox theologian, and a warm opponent of the adversaries of Christianity, though an advanced Rationalist. In the ethical spirit of his time he called into question the supernatural origin and most of the miracles of Scripture; and, after the middle of the century, he excited many doubts on the authenticity of entire books of Scripture by his "free examination of the Canon." After his example, theologians continued to explain away Scripture as only a moral revelation; to disburden religion of its miracles and creeds, and regard it simply as a moral system. Then came two important Biblical scholars—Paulus, with his naturalistic interpretation of the miraculous history; J. G. Eichhorn, a semi-apologetic critic, who, however, has an important relation to modern thought. He is considered by many to be the founder of modern Old Testament criticism, and his "Introduction to the Old Testament" is said to have exercised as much influence on contemporary opinion as Wellhausen's "Prolegomena" in our days. Compared with later critics, he is most cautious and conservative, though he has a clear conception of the Maccabean date of Daniel. His most important work is the development of Astruc's hypothesis of the composite character of Genesis, which has since proved so fruitful. Eichhorn's successor at Jena, Karl D. Ilgen; De Wette, who relaxed from his first position of ardent critic to an orthodox liberalism; and Gesenius, who was coveted by our own Oxford University in 1832, continued the tradition. In 1810 a new centre of activity was created by the foundation of the Berlin University. Schleiermacher, an important orthodox theologian, who was the first professor appointed, marked his appreciation of the rapidly developing system in stating that "the Old Testament was merely the accidental soil in which Christianity was rooted"—it was a premature enunciation of the position which the majority of orthodox divines were ultimately to adopt. De Wette and Neander were also aggregated to the new University. Ewald was the next prominent figure in the critical movement. Like Eichhorn, he was an orthodox but advanced critic, who held aloof from theological quarrels, and continued his investigations with a sincere fearlessness of consequences. In 1823 he opposed both the current theories of the origin of Genesis, which was then the main object of controversy; but modified his position eight years afterwards. He also advanced the theory that the Song of Songs was a sort of popular drama, a cantata describing the victory of true love. The year 1835 was marked by the appearance of Strauss' famous "Leben Jesu," and Vatke's "Biblische Theologie." Vatke was a pronounced Hegelian, and his later speculations are said to have found little favour. His association with the "Fragmentary theory" of Genesis gives him an important place in the development of criticism. Bleek, Hengstenberg, Hupfeld, and F. Delitzsch played the part of foils to the zeal of their more Rationalistic colleagues. Of the latter, Canon Cheyne says that whatever concessions he made to the critics were literally "wrung from him." Riehm was also prominent on the orthodox side, and Reuss did much to popularize the critical theories. Lagarde, Kuenen, Stade, and Wellhausen bring the critical tradition to the actual generation; of the New Testament critics and Christologists we shall speak afterwards. Wellhausen is a typical Rationalist, and the ablest and most influential critic of the modern school. Lagarde, though called one of the founders of the new Hexateuch criticism, remained in the orthodox ranks in an advanced position. Kuenen, the celebrated Dutch critic of Leyden University, was a theologian of firm and reverent faith, but, like Lagarde, his ideal was a pure ethical Theism; he had no sympathy with traditional forms of Christianity, and considered all dogmatic supernaturalism untenable; hence his criticism, ever cautious and fundamentally reverent, was of the most uncompromising character.

In England there was no corresponding development of the critical methods. During the preceding century three theologians had manifested Rationalistic tendencies. Bishop

Warburton had thrown out certain suggestions in connection with Job and the Song of Songs. Bishop Lowth had deviated a little from the traditional view of the prophets, contending that they spoke primarily to their own time; and Dr. A. Geddes had made a direct attack upon the old theory of the Mosaic authorship of the Pentateuch. He held that the Pentateuch had been written or compiled from a number of documents about the time of Solomon in Jerusalem. Dr. Geddes was familiar with the recent speculations on Genesis of his German contemporaries, and his own theory, which differs slightly from Eichhorn's, was taught for a long period in Germany. Westphal calls it the Geddes-Vater theory—it is usually called the "Fragmentary hypothesis," as we shall see. Dr. Geddes was a Roman Catholic priest, but he was suspended from sacerdotal functions when he published his "Critical Remarks on the Hebrew Scriptures" in the year 1800. He boldly announced the first postulate of Rationalistic criticism, which is now almost universally conceded : " Let the father of Hebrew be tried by the same rules of criticism as Greek history."

It would be expected that the good seed which was thus planted on British soil at the beginning of the century would have been carefully cultivated by the semi-Rationalistic school which we have seen to be so active in England even in the first half of this century. In point of fact, the history of criticism in England is almost a perfect blank until the appearance of "Essays and Reviews" in 1861 ; it is relieved only by the appearance of a few unimportant works, such as the "Book of Jasher," by J. W. Donaldson. This sterility, which reflects so little credit on our English universities, now that the results of the brilliant labours of the German scholars are freely accepted within and without the Church, is entirely due to the ecclesiastical and academic authorities.

At the end of the eighteenth century a Cambridge professor, H. Lloyd, meditated a translation of Eichhorn's "Introduction to the Old Testament" that had recently created a profound sensation in Germany. The authorities refused their sanction to the translation, and their opposition led to a decay of the Oriental studies which were absolutely necessary even to keep pace with the learned Germans. Thus it is that neither Hare, nor Dr. Arnold, nor Jowett, nor Dean Stanley, with all their liberality of feeling and breadth of mind, contributed to the advancing science.

But in 1864 a powerful and successful effort was made to cast off the irksome restrictions under which the Broad Church chafed. Dr. Williams, as we have seen, introduced B. Bunsen's critical theories to English readers, and made a bold defence of the entire German movement. Hardly had the intellectual world realized the significance of this new offence of the semi-Rationalists than Bishop Colenso's "Pentateuch and Book of Joshua Critically Examined" came to confirm the impression; and it was followed, after the favourable decisions of the Privy Council, by a series of subversive speculations on the whole of the Old Testament. England was now inflamed with the controversy, and more than 300 replies to Colenso's first book appeared. Colenso did little more than give a "timid adhesion" to the speculations of the Germans, and his own theories have met with little approval. Besides emphasizing the innumerable contradictions and impossibilities of the text, he rejected entirely the orthodox notions of the authorship of the books of the Old Testament, supporting the composite character and the late date of the Pentateuch and the historical books. He adopts the hypothesis of Vatke on the post-exilic origin of the Levitical legislation, which, he says, "strikes a death-blow at the whole system of priestcraft." He teaches that the early history of the Old Testament is purely legendary; that the patriarchs and even Moses were probably mythical; that Israel was not an object of special divine choice; that Jehovah was the sun-god of the Phœnicians, with which the Israelites became acquainted about the time of the exile; that the "Exodus" is a distorted account of the expulsion of the shepherd-kings; and an infinity of equally revolutionary propositions. The learned and exhaustive treatises of the South African bishop did much towards familiarizing the nation with the new conception of Scripture. About the same time appeared S. Davidson's "Introduction to the Old Testament," also relating with some degree of approval the conclusions of the critics on the Hexateuch. Much service was also rendered by the Jewish theologian, Dr. Kalisch, who came to England as a political refugee in 1848. He agrees generally with the higher critics, and helped to propagate their theories in England.

In our own days the purified conception of the Bible is widely accepted among Biblical scholars, and is being rapidly propagated among the rank and file of the orthodox Churches by members of their own clergy. Not only such professed theological sceptics as Dr. Momerie and Mr. Craufurd advocate it, but some of the most influential writers and teachers of the Anglican communion are in substantial agreement with the most advanced critics, though they resist the inferences which the critics draw from their theories. A work has been recently published by Deans Farrar and Fremantle, and a number of influential clergymen and laymen, which advocates a "discreet" use of the critical theories even in the education of the young, and evinces a perfect resignation to the new presentation of the historic volume. Mr. Stead has elicited from several bishops the opinion that the time has come to incorporate many of the new views into ordinary Biblical education. The Biblical articles in that universal educator, the "Encyclopædia Britannica," are by the most advanced scholars—the most important title, the "Pentateuch," has been entrusted to Wellhausen himself, the "Prophets" to Canon Cheyne, and the majority to W. Robertson Smith. Cheyne, Canon of the Established Church, and Oriel professor of Interpretation of the Holy Scripture, adopting an attitude of perfect candour and fearlessness which does him credit, has come to accept, and ardently propagates, the views of Kuenen and Wellhausen—except in their application to the religious history of Israel; he is entirely free from, and earnestly deprecates, the spirit of timidity and compromise which enfeebles the efforts of most of his colleagues. W. Robertson Smith, the late Arabic professor of Cambridge and an intimate friend of Wellhausen, in spite of his taint of compromise and occasional hesitation, has conducted an effective propaganda of the higher criticism. Professor Driver, though fettered by a more direct anti-critical influence, admits "whatever is vitally important," as Cheyne says. Even Professor Sayce, of whom Canon Cheyne writes "for the sake of historical truth let those who read Professor Sayce be on their guard," and who is the last support of the anti-critical party, largely accepts the new analysis of the Old Testament, and often adds most destructive evidence from his Assyriological researches. Making due allowance for the timidity and compromise which always characterize the attitude of the clergy in the transition from opposition to acceptance, we may confidently regard the victory of the higher criticism as decisive. All the contentions of the critics are not admitted, except by those theologians who succeed in pursuing grammatico-historical exegesis quite apart from theology; but sufficient is admitted to justify the assertion that the Christian conception of the Bible has been revolutionized. We shall throughout distinguish between the unaccepted and the received views of the purely Rationalistic critics; but an independent and unbiassed mind will naturally prefer to follow the guidance of non-theological scholars.

The inquiry has been chiefly directed to the Pentateuch and the prophets in the Old Testament, and it is here especially that the revolutionary character of the analysis is discerned. In both cases the compromising tendency of theological critics is to be guarded against by the candid inquirer, on account of the possible dogmatic consequences of any change in that direction. However, the whole ground of the Canon has been laboriously covered by the German critics. In the case of nearly every book the result has been fatal to the traditional belief, and in most cases the new doctrine is in startling contrast to the old. Many of the hypotheses are still only provisional, and a *résumé* of the results of the higher criticism is not yet a collection of stereotyped conclusions. At the same time, so many of the most important conclusions have been ratified by general acceptance that they may be duly registered as final acquisitions to science. It will be impossible, as a rule, even to glance at the process of reasoning by which the conclusions have been reached; but a fuller exposition of the Hexateuch controversy, the first and most ardent struggle, will throw some light upon the vast labour which has been expended, and the constant control of hostile forces, in arriving at definite results. To the Pentateuch, or five books which form the *Torah*, the first section of the Jewish canon, it has been found necessary to add the Book of Joshua, which continues the early narrative, and shares the peculiar composite structure of the Pentateuch; hence the writers now invariably speak of the Hexateuch, or group of six books. The first object of the critics was to refute the traditional belief in the Mosaic authorship of the Pentateuch. That belief is now almost confined to the Church of Rome, and is only defended by the more erudite scholars of that body in deference to a despotic reactionary authority. The second point of the critics was to institute a searching analysis of the text, by which they discovered its composite and comparatively recent character, and were finally enabled to reproduce the original synthesis of the narrative. The history of the process is extremely interesting and instructive.

Although there had been sporadic deviations from the traditional view of the Pentateuch during the preceding two centuries, the modern controversy may be said to date from the middle of the last century. In the year 1753 a French physician, named Astruc, published a work at Brussels entitled "Conjectures sur les mémoires originaux dont il parait que Moyse s'est servi pour composer le livre de la Génèse." He had noticed that the two names of God which occur in the Hebrew text—Elohim and Jahve, (Yahweh, or Jehovah, as the second is commonly read)—are not used indiscriminately, but seem to reveal the presence of two distinct writers who are severally characterized by them. He surmised that Moses had had two more ancient documents before him in composing Genesis. Thus was vaguely started the "Documentary hypothesis," around which all subsequent criticism has centred. Smith says: "That the way in which the two names are used can only be due to difference of authorship is now generally admitted." Astruc's suggestion was, however, treated with contempt in those days, and met with the usual theological stigma—"*systema ineptissimum conjecturarum*," such as is applied to the theories of Kuenen and Wellhausen to-day. A few years afterwards Eichhorn revived the teaching of Astruc, and strengthened it by other linguistic considerations in his "Einleitung." Michaelis also patronized it. Like Astruc, Eichhorn at first sustained that Moses was the compiler; but, as Mr. Addis forcibly urges, the Mosaic authorship is inevitably relinquished when the analysis is extended to the whole of the Hexateuch. It is impossible to think that any man wrote contradictory accounts of his own life, and systematically employed two different styles in his own narrative. Eichhorn had a powerful influence on the rising Biblical scholars, and they immediately applied themselves to the problem. Ilgen, Stähelin, Gramberg, and Kelle followed him with more or less fidelity.

In the meantime Geddes, in England, had suggested what is known as the "Fragmentary hypothesis," which regarded the Pentateuch as originating in a series of old laws and fragments of laws collected in the time of David and Solomon, which formed the basis of the actual Deuteronomy. The theory was adopted by Vater, and superseded the former hypothesis in Germany for some time. At length De Wette initiated the "Supplementary hypothesis," which supposes one document to be the basis of the Pentateuch, and that supplementary additions have been made to it, and particulars of a much later date incorporated into it. Instead of considering Deuteronomy to be the earliest stratum of the Pentateuch literature, he makes it the most recent, and assigns it to the age of Josiah. He considers the Elohistic document (in which the name Elohim occurs) the most ancient of the three—Elohistic, Jehovistic, and Deuteronomic. This theory held the ground until the speculations of Hupfeld in 1853, but is now almost antiquated. It is still held by Schrader, though Schrader is better known as an Assyriologist than a critic. Bleek, who followed De Wette, annexed the book of Joshua to the Pentateuch, and thus started the inquiry on the whole Hexateuch; and Ewald traced the two documents throughout. The problem of the respective ages of the documents led to an infinite diversity of opinions, as was natural in the yet imperfect state of speculation. All, however, agreed that the Elohistic document was the "Grund-schrift," or fundamental document which was used by the Jahvist, and supplemented by the Deuteronomist.

About the middle of the century Hupfeld made the important discovery that there were two Elohistic writers; that the Jahvist and the elder Elohist had been combined by a second Elohist, and he added that a fourth writer reunited the whole; but the latter point was immediately corrected by Nöldeke. As the theory now stood, therefore, there were four documents constituting the Hexateuch—namely, the Jahvist (J), and the second Elohist (E^2), which were welded at an early date; the Deuteronomist

(D), and a fourth, which has received various titles—the Grund-schrift (Tuch), the Book of Origins (Ewald), the Annalistic writer (Schrader), the first Elohist (E^1), and the Priestly Code (P.C.); it is now usually called by the last name. Kuenen gave his weighty adhesion to the theory of Graf and Hupfeld in its bold outlines, and it received the assent of Colenso and Wellhausen and all subsequent critics. The date and the extent of the respective documents were still a matter of grave discussion and endless differences; but an important stage had been reached, and the general thesis of the origin of Genesis from the four documents mentioned received almost universal acceptance.

Before proceeding to state more clearly the conclusion which has been adopted, it is well to note the unity and consistent growth which is perceptible in the apparently ceaseless variation. There are reviewers (of the *Quarterly Review* type) who are content to reject the conclusions of the critics by an appeal to the contradictory opinions which have been patronized at successive stages of the history of Biblical criticism. But, as Mr. Addis remarks, "we only need some real knowledge of the course which criticism has followed to perceive that the general knowledge of the documents which compose the Hexateuch has been gaining ground step by step," and that there has been "an amazing growth of unanimity." It is no longer wise to reproach the doctrine of biological evolution with the varied treatment it received in its growth from Lamarck, Darwin, and Spencer, or the nebular hypothesis with the variety of forms it assumed in the hands of Descartes, Kant, Laplace, and Flammarion. Such reproaches do not aid the elucidation of a truth. But, in point of fact, there has been a uniform progress amid the prolific growth of Pentateuch theories during the century. Astruc and Eichhorn's idea of Elohistic and Jahvistic documents perseveres throughout. The extension of the analysis to the rest of the Pentateuch, and ultimately to Joshua, by Bleek, was a legitimate step. De Wette's separation of Deuteronomy from the rest of the Pentateuch, on account of its distinctive style, was a second stage of growth. Even the date he assigned to Deuteronomy is retained by modern criticism. Ewald's tracing of the two documents throughout the Hexateuch was a step in advance. The Fragmentary hypothesis, which was correct in extending the analysis beyond Genesis and the beginning of Exodus, and in rejecting the idea that Genesis consisted of documents used by Moses, erred only in not perceiving the possible reduction to a common source of many of its "fragments." This error, or oversight, was corrected by the third hypothesis; the modern theory completed the progress by its discovery of a subdivision of one of the documents. Thus the successive hypotheses are not disjointed and conflicting systems, but consistent stages of growth of one central idea, around which innumerable personalities are clustered. And the Grundschrift, Book of Origins, Annalistic Writer, Elohist, Book of the Four Covenants, and Priestly Code, or Writer, are so many titles, suggested by different aspects, of one and the same document—the one which serves as a framework, and gives order and unity to the whole Hexateuch.

It is possible, therefore, at the present day to offer a decisive analysis of the Hexateuch as the accepted result of the long controversy. The traditional notion, that Moses wrote the earlier books of Scripture as sole and inspired author, is entirely obsolete. Even Professor Sayce admits that "about the general fact of the composite character of the Pentateuch competent critics of all schools are now agreed."* The few who still contend for a Mosaic authorship admit that it is a compilation, and that it has been much modified subsequently. It is significant to note that almost all who cling to the Mosaic authorship and editorship are persuaded that its denial has grave theological implications. In the second place, there is unanimity among the critics with regard to the character of the documents which compose the Hexateuch. Four main documents have been unanimously recognised—the Deuteronomist, the Priestly Writer, the Jahvist, and the Elohist. The principles on which the several documents have been traced in the exceedingly complex structure of the Pentateuch are numerous and effective. Not only the curious duality of names which was the first to be remarked, and manifest differences of style and lexicology, and of psychological assumption, come to the aid of the analysts, but the final synthesis has been so crude that the narrative contains numerous

* "The Higher Criticism and the Verdict of the Monuments."

anachronisms, omissions, repetitions, and contradictions which offer an infallible criterion. Indeed, if doctrinal prepossessions were not in the way, the composite hypothesis would be welcomed by theologians as a much more natural solution of Biblical difficulties than the precarious modes of reconciliation which have hitherto calmed the believing conscience. The defects of the Old Testament literature are obviously due to the clumsiness or indifference of the final Redactor. The varieties of style are, of course, appreciable only to the Hebraist; but the "chronological monstrosities," as Mr. Addis calls them, have been a stumbling-block to all generations, and the virtual and even actual contradictions of the narrative are patent and numerous. Thus, in the legislative portion, there are three codes of laws that completely ignore each other's existence. "To say nothing of the remarkable divergence of style," says even the timid Dr. Driver, "Deuteronomy conflicts with the legislation of Exodus–Numbers in a manner that would not be credible were the legislator in both one and the same." Again, in the book of the Covenant (Exodus xx.) sacrifice is permitted at many shrines; in Deuteronomy only one shrine is recognised. In the book of the Covenant there is no mention of a priestly race; in Deuteronomy the tribe of Levites appears; in the Priestly Writer the sons of Aaron rise above even the Levites. And, in matters of fact, contradictions are much more numerous and less easily explained away. There are two contradictory accounts of the Creation; there are two divergent accounts of the flood; there are two distinct accounts of Joseph's history; there are discordant traditions of the origin of proper names, such as Beersheba and Bethel. The name Yahweh is known to Eve, and familiar to the patriarchs, according to J.; it is revealed for the first time to Moses during his exile among the Midianites, according to E.[2]; it is expressly said to be unknown to the patriarchs, and first revealed to Moses on his return to Egypt, by P.W. In E. the tent of meeting is said to have been outside the camp and left to the charge of an Ephraimite; in P.C. the tent is said to have been in the centre of the camp, and to have been guarded by a double cordon—the inner of priests, and the outer of Levites. There are two different accounts of the sending of manna and the quails, and two of the sending of the spies into the promised land.* And when we find that throughout these divergent narratives there is a consistent and marked diversity of style, it is impossible not to regard them as distinct threads which have been unskilfully woven. The task of the critic in disentangling them is comparatively easy.

Moreover, there is a general agreement among critics with regard to the character and relative extent of the documents. The documents J. and E. cannot be easily distinguished throughout; but, as all admit that they were combined at an early date by a "Harmonist," it is usual to analyze the Hexateuch into the three main portions—J.-E., D, and P. C.; "in the limits of these three, critics of different schools are practically agreed," says Dr. Cheyne. The Jahvist and Elohist were historians, according to the fashion of their remote time; they collected the traditions, myths, and legends (as we shall see presently) which were handed down in their own nation or in surrounding peoples. Their work differs only from the mythical early literature of all the great nations of antiquity in that it had a monotheistic and more ethical character. The hortatory style of the Deuteronomist (whose work does not begin at the commencement of the actual Deuteronomy, and continues into the book of Joshua) facilitates his recognition; his document was practically marked out by Hollenberg in 1874. He is the apostle of law, describes the new law-giving and hortatory discourses of Moses, and extols Joshua as a pious hero who observed the law. The work of the Priestly Writer is also dissected with comparative ease and unanimity. He combines the functions of legislative and historical writer; but it is clear that his history is entirely subservient to his sacerdotal purpose. He is a *Levitical* legislator; "his dry annalistic history," says Addis, "which prepares the way for an elaborate ritualistic code, extends from the first verse of Genesis almost to the end of Joshua." It was dissected out by Nöldeke as early as 1869. His history is entirely constructed with a view to legislation, and his legislation is entirely religious; his religion is, moreover, highly ritualistic, hence he attaches an importance to the priesthood which is

---

* *Vide* "Documents of the Hexateuch," Introduction, by W. E. Addis, who gives an imposing catalogue of contradictions, etc.

unknown in the rest of the Pentateuch. Indeed, so patent is the purpose of his work that even Dr. Driver regretfully admits that "it is difficult to escape the conclusion"—however much one may wish—"that the representation of P. contains elements not in the ordinary sense of the word historical."

So far there is unanimity among critics, orthodox and heterodox; numerous editions of the Hexateuch are now published in which the various elements are printed in different types or in different colours, and Mr. Addis's valuable work presents to English readers a perfectly detached and continuous version of the constituent documents. The analysis, worked out step by step in the teeth of a century of Christian prejudice and obloquy, is one of the finest literary triumphs of the Rationalistic spirit, and one of its most brilliant contributions to positive science; it is already being claimed by divines (as in the case of the theory of evolution) as a quasi-providential revelation. Orthodox critics have succeeded in readjusting their doctrinal tenets to the new analysis with comparative ease; when, however, we come to the question of the order and date of the documents, to the *synthesis* of the Hexateuch, the strain is much more appreciated, and there is less unanimity. Here, again, it is significant to note that those who candidly lay aside their theological notions in applying themselves to criticism, like Cheyne and Robertson Smith, consider the positions of Kuenen and Stade and Wellhausen to be unassailable.

With regard to the date of D. and J.-E., as Wellhausen says, there is tolerable agreement. The compound historical document J.-E. is the oldest of the three. It must have been written some time before the destruction of the Northern Kingdom, for the Elohist clearly wrote in the Northern Kingdom. A general consensus of critics places them both in the golden age of Hebrew literature, between 850 and 750 B.C., many centuries after the death of Moses. It is allowed, however, that they contain older fragments, although leading critics cannot admit the Mosaic authorship of even the Decalogue in its actual form. The date of the Deuteronomist and his age relative to P.C. (especially the latter point) is a present subject of controversy between the "advanced" and the "moderate" critics. In both cases there are doctrinal implications. The general opinion of the critics, with whom Cheyne agrees, assigns it to the reign of Josiah. Ewald, Riehm, Bleek, and a few others place its composition a century earlier, in the time of Manasseh; but "the ruling critical opinion," as Delitzsch confesses, attributes it to the High Priest Hilkiah, about 621 B.C. The fact that it differs conspicuously in style, and conflicts with the legislation of the Priestly Code, completely negatives the old notion that it came from the inspired pen of Moses with the other books of the Pentateuch. That it cannot be older than Hezekiah seems certain, because it maintains that sacrifice can only be offered at the central shrine; whereas, down to the time of Hezekiah, prophets and pious kings had sacrificed in the "high places." The book, which is said (2 Kings xxii.) to have been "discovered" in the eighteenth year of Josiah, is recognised to be Deuteronomy, and critics are almost unanimous that it was actually composed at, or very shortly previous to, that date by the High Priest who "discovered" it. The priests had meditated a reform of the cultus, and they secretly composed the book, foisted it upon Moses, and pretended to discover it with the well-known dramatic circumstances. Such is the theory, admitted even by the best orthodox critics, of the origin of this book of Scripture. Yet even here the theological spirit displays its wonted fertility. There was no "forgery," not even a "*pia fraus.*" The book was Mosaic in substance, at least, and the transaction will stand Canon Gore's test of forgery (drawn up with an eye to this incident)—"to find out whether the writer of a particular book could have afforded to disclose the method and circumstances of its production." Moreover, the book is inspired. Hilkiah was inspired by God to make a bold *coup* for reform, and the "finding" of Deuteronomy in the ark (where he had put it himself) was the result.*

But a more important controversy is still raging, though it is decidedly on the wane, with regard to the origin of the Priestly Code. Until a comparatively recent date, the P.C. was considered the earliest of the three documents. Many

---

* It is interesting to find that it was an English theological writer who saw for the first time (in 1739) that Deuteronomy was a product of the seventh century B.C.

reasons were alleged, but it was really owing to the "supplementary hypothesis," which had made P.C. (the major portion of Exodus, Leviticus, and Numbers) the *"grundschrift"* of the whole Hexateuch. Graf at length succeeded in changing the opinion, or in reviving the old opinion of Vatke, that the Levitical legislation was of post-exilian origin. Kuenen supported and enforced the change, and it became the accepted theory. Colenso was of the same opinion. It is the common opinion of the German critics— Wellhausen, Kuenen, Stade, Schultz, Kayser, Smend, Budde, etc.—and is shared by Kalisch, Cheyne, Robertson Smith, and others in England. Robertson Smith speaks of the "demonstration, for such I venture to call it," that the Priestly Legislation did not exist before the exile; and Cheyne thinks that the arguments are "irresistible to a fresh mind." The chief argument lies in the finished ritual and sacerdotalism of the P.W., and the novelty of his doctrines. Throughout Deuteronomy and the rest of Hebrew literature priests and Levites are not distinguished —all Levites may be priests. In P.C. there is a sharp distinction drawn between the priests (the descendants of Aaron) and the Levites who occupy a subordinate position. In P.C., also, the hierarchy leads up to a High Priest of an importance which is unknown in the other documents. His entire scheme—the graduated hierarchy, the elaborate ritual, the strict centralization of cult, the number of festivals, the income of priests and Levites, etc.—points to a later period of development. Hence it is the general opinion of the critics that it was composed during and after the exile, and incorporated with the rest of the Hexateuch about the time of Ezra, about 444 B.C. (though there are later additions). Dillman and a few others would substitute the precarious hypothesis that it was composed about 800 B.C., but not published, because it received no royal or public sanction. It remained in sacerdotal circles, and was at length much amplified and produced by priests who remained at Babylon after the captivity. There seems little reason for the hypothesis (beyond the desire to avoid unpleasant theological consequences); and, as Wellhausen points out, the three documents naturally correspond to the three periods of the religious history of the nation:—(1) To the period before Josiah, when there was sacrifice in the "high places," etc., the J.-E. document naturally belongs; (2) to the reforming reign of Josiah and centralization of cultus we may securely refer Deuteronomy; (3) after the exile, when all traditions had been fatally uprooted, we find the natural opportunity for priestly innovations.

From these data the important inference is drawn that the history of the Hebrew religion is not a supernatural exception to the law of evolution, but that it is a perfectly natural and ordinary growth. This point is, of course, the rock that divides the stream of criticism; but, if we take a purely scientific estimate of the three documents, in that character and of that period which the vast majority of the critics assign to them, we are constrained to regard them as marks of the successive stages through which the religion has passed. The early narrative depicts a period without priest, or temple, or ritual—if it does not indeed lead us back to a pre-monotheistic period, as the " advanced " critics maintain; Deuteronomy marks an early stage of the growth of sacerdotalism, and of the decay of religion; the later writing describes the complete inauguration of an elaborate ritual and hierarchy. Every religion, even Christianity, has had a similar growth; to scientific critics, unembarrassed with doctrinal prepossessions, the unveiling of Israel's growth was but a confirmation of an anticipation which general principles had led them to form. Unfortunately for historical science, it was brought once more into conflict with an important religious doctrine; Christendom was already convinced that Hebrew religion had not been a natural growth, but that its fabric had been revealed and ordained by Jehovah amid the thunders of Sinai, and its principles committed to writing and partially carried out (especially in the creation of the Aaronic priesthood) by Moses himself. That belief has been completely undermined; even orthodox critics (such as Robertson Smith) admit that the religious institutions of the Hebrews have been a gradual growth, the centralization of worship a natural development, the rise of the Aaronic family to power a secondary growth out of the institution of Levites in the wilderness. They maintain that this process has been presided over and directed by an all-ruling providence, and "a triumph of spiritual religion over opposing forces;" that, therefore, no real doctrinal sacrifice is involved in its acceptance. But the consequences of the theory are too grave to be lightly swept aside, and every effort of modern priests to palliate and sanctify the action of the writers of the P.C. only shows the utter unsoundness and unreliability of sacerdotal conduct in all time and place; they have a standard of rectitude in pursuing their own ends (so intimately connected with those of Jehovah) which is repellent to the lay mind. The priestly writers found a convenient opportunity to gratify their ambition after the Babylonian exile, and they literally forged the Pentateuch in the name of Moses, just as Hilkiah had forged Deuteronomy; the test of forgery used by Canons Gore and Cheyne will hardly satisfy the unecclesiastical conscience—certainly not a legal mind. The whole system is the outgrowth of priestly ambition and avarice; and the whole system of Mosaism, in which Christendom devoutly believed so long, is a vast clerical fraud, in which some of the venerated figures of the Old Testament are deeply involved.

Moreover, it follows that almost the whole of the "historical" section of the Old Testament is absolutely unreliable. Dr. Driver feebly remarks that much of P.C.'s work is "not in the ordinary sense historical;" the truth is that he has written entirely with a purpose of glorifying the ritual and the clergy, and when an Oriental writer is inspired with any such motive we know the value of his statements. It is useless to contend that "we must not judge such ancient documents by modern canons of criticism," for the Old Testament has been rigidly enforced upon humanity by the Churches as historical in the modern sense. It is a hopeless mass of myths and legends of uncertain origin. The stories of the earlier document are Hebraized versions of popular myths of all nations; the patriarchs are as mythical as Romulus and Remus. Deuteronomy and the Priestly Code may or may not possess fragments of sound history, but their discreditable origin alienates all respect; and, as we shall see, the books of Judges, Samuel, and Kings have suffered from the same influence, and Chronicles were forged by the priests as literally as the Levitical legislation. The further difficulty which arises with regard to Christ's ascription of the Pentateuch to Moses will be considered later.

It is necessary to add that a new force has appeared

which bears upon the critical problem, and from which many of the anti-critics are expecting a rehabilitation of their fallen theories. The deciphering of ancient monuments has given rise to the new sciences of Assyriology, Egyptology, etc., and some of their most prominent representatives, as Sayce and Schrader, have taken up an attitude of opposition to the critics. In the first place, it must be noted that the evidence of the monuments militates against the old orthodox view of Scripture much more than against the views of Cheyne and Wellhausen; the S. P. C. K. is driven to the questionable expedient of using Sayce against the critics, while rejecting the more important of his conclusions, which are very advanced. But, in point of fact, the result of Professor Sayce's achievements does not seriously affect the critical position—does not at all affect its main points. Mr. Sayce contends that his evidence throws back the date of many of the sources of the Hexateuch, and sometimes corroborates the Old Testament where the critics had refused its testimony; it would, therefore, tend to restore its historical credit. But, from a purely critical point of view, the new evidence makes little or no difference to the problem. Archæological research *has* confirmed the Scripture narrative in some passages, but it has equally negatived it in others; the narrative is, therefore, as useless as ever in itself, without the confirmation of the monuments in detail. That the higher critics have erred in several points is of little significance; if they had been convicted of such enormous errors as the Church has been guilty of in teaching the Mosaic authorship of the Pentateuch, and the inspired character of the historical books of the Old Testament, we should have grave reason to distrust their methods. And then Mr. Sayce's proposed new analysis of the early books into Babylonian, Egyptian, Aramaic, Edomite, and Canaanitish elements neither conflicts with the literary analysis, nor restores confidence in the narrative; the fact that the narrative of the creation is a purified copy of a Babylonian epic, that the day of seven weeks and the Sabbath comes from Babylon, that Eden was the great plain of Babylon, that the Hebrews most probably borrowed from the Babylonians the notions of the tree of life, of the cherubim, of the creation of woman out of man, of the fall by eating the forbidden fruit, of the deluge in all its details, that the history of Joseph is probably a copy of an Egyptian novel, etc., is rather a welcome illustration of the critical theory. How the dogmas of Inspiration, the Fall, etc., are reconciled with the new evidence is another question; the mere fact that the Jahvist or the Elohist made use of Babylonian bricks and Egyptian papyri (or remote copies of them) in writing his narrative is interesting, but is far from restoring confidence in Genesis. The stories remain myths and legends, which it would be weakness of mind to accept as truths; once for all, they are not revelations made to Moses. And the defects which Mr. Sayce finds in the historical books, the "foreshortening of chronological perspective" (as he mildly puts it), the victories exaggerated and defeats suppressed, etc., do but confirm the critical theory of their origin. There is no contradiction between literary and archæological results; when the two work harmoniously, the result will be a fuller and more satisfactory development of the critical scheme.

The labours of the critics on the Hexateuch, which have been described at length, will serve to illustrate their methods throughout the whole of the Bible. It will be impossible to enter in detail upon the controversies over each book of the canon; we can only give the results which have obtained general assent. The traditional belief in the authorship of the several books has been falsified in almost every instance, and the books have been thrown back to a much later date than Christendom had imagined. The authority of the historical books has been entirely destroyed—no single statement can be accepted without archæological confirmation. Many books which were formerly thought historical are proved to be pure fiction. It will be useful to take a brief survey of the canon.

The books of Judges, Samuel, and Kings, from which we had been taught ancient history for many generations, are now quite denuded of credibility, if not of utility. The Rev. Lyman Abbott* says: "How far those books which are historical in form have a historical basis of truth we cannot now judge." The opinion marks a step of progress, but it is hardly correct. We *can* judge; even Mr. Sayce, who has given them all the support which a zealous and

---

* In "The Bible and the Child," by Dean Farrar and associates.

fertile imagination could derive from the cuneiform inscriptions, admits that they form a "defective" and "inaccurate" history. They consist of "a series of extracts and abstracts from various [unauthenticated] sources which have been worked over from time to time by successive editors and freely handled by copyists" (Robertson Smith). The older narratives go back to the time of the Assyrian monarchy, but they have been so tampered with by successive editors, especially by the final Redactor in the exilic period, that, if they had any original value, it has become an uncertain quantity. The whole was revised from the priestly standpoint, hence we are not to look for history in them, but, as Dr. Driver admits, "the philosophy of history"—from a sacerdotal point of view.

The books of Chronicles (together with Ezra and Nehemiah, in which the narrative is continued, and which are in the same style) are placed by the advanced critics in the same category as Exodus, Numbers, and Leviticus. They are forgeries in favour of the extension of priestly power and the ritualism of the temple. Ezra and Nehemiah may incorporate original memoirs, but the whole was written about the close of the Persian, and beginning of the Greek, period (fourth century B.C.). All critics agree that they are of no more value than the other sacerdotal elements of the Old Testament; they are utterly untrustworthy. The writer is either a priest or a tool of the priesthood—"not so much an historian," says R. Smith, "as a Levitical preacher;" he colours all events, and forces them into harmony with the Priestly Code, and writes fictitious genealogies of Levitical descent. Mr. Sayce's defence of him is characteristic. He says the writer is more trustworthy than critics allow; but, at the same time, completely destroys his credit. His chronology (according to Professor Sayce) is "an artificial scheme which breaks down before the facts of contemporary monuments;" between Archbishop Usher's version of it (the best of many) and Assyriology there is "an irreconcilable difference." "His use of documents is uncritical, his inferences are unsound, and he makes everything subserve his theory. His ecclesiastical tone cannot fail to strike us;" "from the historical point of view his unsupported statements must be received with great caution;" "he did not possess that sense of exactitude which we require in a modern historian," etc. However, Canon Cheyne assures his readers that the books may still be regarded as "inspired"—in the sense that a good sermon is inspired. Most men will admit that the books are "inspired," though not from heaven.

Ruth, Esther, Tobit, and Judith (the two latter are received as canonical by the Church of Rome) may be classed together as a group of pious stories with no appreciable historical value. "The decipherment of the cuneiform inscriptions," says Professor Sayce, "has finally destroyed all claim on the part of the books of Tobit and Judith to be considered as history;" and he extends the statement to the fragments of Susanna and Bel and the dragon. The Anglican Church is, therefore, to be congratulated on its exclusion of them from the canon, for they have certainly no ethical value. Ruth, according to Canon Cheyne, "is practically as imaginative as the book of Tobit;" it is of post-exilic composition. Esther is another work of pious fiction, which, at the most, may be founded on a semi-historical legend (the most Professor Sayce can claim). It was probably written by a Jew in the third century B.C., to whom the customs and names of the Persians loomed very indistinct through "the mists of antiquity" (Sayce). The name Esther itself (which has become, on account of the Biblical heroine, a favourite with Christian maidens) is really the great goddess of impurity, Istar (the Astarte of the Syrians, and Aphrodite of the Greeks). The name could not have been borne by a woman, except in combination. Mordecai, the name given to the devout Hebrew, means "devoted to Merodach," the Babylonian god.

The book of Job is now generally admitted to be, in its present form, post-exilic. Cheyne says it most probably belongs to the Persian period, and that it is due to a number of different authors. That it is not an historical narrative is, of course, conceded by all. Cheyne thinks it probably founded on one of the simple folk-stories, and Sayce is inclined to believe it was originally a genuine specimen of North Arabian or Edomite literature which passed into Jewish hands. When we come to the Song of Songs and Ecclesiastes, says Cheyne, "the difficulties of theories of inspiration are still greater." The Song of Songs is, indeed, one of the most incongruous elements of the "inspired" book. Its inspiration is purely sensual and erotic. "In it, according to most critics," says Robertson Smith, "the pure love of the Shulamite for her betrothed is depicted as victorious over the seductions of Solomon and his harem." It is a beautiful love-song, a kind of lyric-drama, without any consciousness of allegory on the writer's part, and without any known basis of fact. The gravity with which we monks used to recite it in our choir, applying the most sensual and (from the modern point of view) indecent passages to the mother of Christ and to his spouse, the Church, is a curious instance of the perversity of superstition. It is post-exilic in origin (Cheyne), many centuries more recent than Solomon. The so-called Proverbs of Solomon are also "not at all Solomonic, though they may contain some of his sayings" (Robertson Smith), and Cheyne speaks of the "worthless tradition of Solomonic authorship." He says that "in final arrangement they are almost certainly post-exilic," and some parts of the book certainly. He adds that the other proverbial books of the Old Testament are certainly later than 538. Ecclesiastes is a work of the Greek period. Kuenen puts it about 200 B.C., about forty years before the Maccabean rising, and he is generally followed.

With regard to the psalms, the principal concern of the higher critics has been to test the accuracy of their titular inscriptions, and discover their true date and authorship. As is found to be the case with nearly all the books of the Old Testament, the titles and the traditions of authorship are entirely wrong. Instead of David being the leading composer of the psalms, there is not a single one that can be confidently attributed to him. All admit that the vast majority of the so-called Davidic psalms are certainly not by David; they "belong to different periods of Israelitish history" (Driver), and Canon Cheyne is inclined to agree with the "advanced" critics that the whole psalter is post-exilic, and at the most may contain a few Davidic elements. Robertson Smith, in his eagerness to enable theologians to retain traditional terminology, can only say that "the so-called psalms of David may come from a collection in which there were psalms of David." The 110th psalm, which Christ expressly attributes to David (Mark xii. 37; Luke xx. 42 and 44), was only written nearly one thousand years after the death of David, and then not in prophetic allusion to the Messiah, but in honor of Simon the Maccabee. The fifty-first psalm, so universally attributed to the penitent David, was, says Robertson Smith, "obviously composed during the destruction of the temple"—most critics think it much later. The first book or collection of psalms (containing the so-called Davidic) seems to have been made in the days of Nehemiah and Ezra; the second and third (containing the Korahites and Asaphites) are much later, as a collection. The fourth and fifth books run down to the Maccabean period, to which many of them (44, 74, 79, 83, etc.) belong.

One of the most important sections—perhaps the most important section—of the Old Testament, in the eyes of the Christian world, has been the collection of prophetical books. The existence of definite prophecies has always been relied upon as one of the most cogent demonstrations of the divinity of Christ, and it was thought that nothing could be clearer than the Messianic predictions of the four major and twelve minor prophets. The notion of prediction has been always regarded as the essential characteristic of the prophet, and it was held that the Messianic revelation, which began vaguely in Genesis, reached an unmistakeable degree of clearness and definition in Isaiah and Daniel. At the present day, however, the orthodox notion of a prophet has undergone a complete metamorphosis. "The predictive element," says Robertson Smith, "received undue prominence, and withdrew attention from the influence of the prophets on the religious life of their time." We are told that they were the "leaders of a great development," that their principal concern was with the present, not with the future; and hence that "there is no reason to think that a prophet ever received a revelation which was not spoken directly and pointedly to his own time." The truth is, of course, that the higher criticism has completely revolutionized the traditional conception of the prophets, and theologians are adapting their tenets to the irresistible conclusions of the critics. All competent orthodox critics now admit that each of the so-called Messianic predictions finds a sufficient explanation in the political circumstances of the period at which it was written. They leave a margin, of course, for their Christian readers to indulge in thoughts of secondary applications of texts; but, from the point of view of positive science, there is absolutely no reason to see a predictive element in any part of the Old Testament. Indeed, "*the* Messiah" (with a definite article) is not an Old Testament phrase at all; it has been read into it. The word Messiah (properly Māshiah), which means "the anointed one," is the ordinary title of the human king. Then, also, the integrity and early date of the prophecies have been shown to be delusive. In fact, some of the prophets have been reduced to myths. How much written prophecy may have existed before the exile is a difficult question; the earliest certainly do not go beyond the eighth century. In any case, all were re-edited after the exile when the scattered remnants of prophecies from a multitude of anonymous writers were collected into a number of books, to which the names of the prophets were given. As Robertson Smith says, "the collections of all remains of ancient prophecies, digested into the four books named from Isaiah, Jeremiah, Ezechiel, and the twelve minor prophets, were not formed till after the time of Ezra, 250 years at least after the death of Isaiah." The higher critics discovered the composite or mosaic character of the books, and were enabled to correct the traditional view of their origin.

Thus, in the prophecy of Isaiah, it was soon discovered that the last twenty-two chapters were by an entirely different writer—a "great unknown prophet" about the time of the Babylonian Captivity; "they cannot be understood in a natural and living way except by looking at them from the historical standpoint of the exile," says Dr. Driver. The whole chronological order of the book is confused, so that it has clearly been redacted by an incompetent later editor, who inserted many fragments which belonged neither to the real nor to the deutero-Isaiah. Thus, the "Messianic" prediction in ii. 2-4 is probably a post-exilic text; so also the "prediction" of the root of Jesse (xi. 10). And the "predictions" which are assigned to Isaiah have lost all supernatural character. He was not only a prophet or religious teacher, but he was an able politician; he shows a clear appreciation of the dangers of the situation, and often gives a shrewd forecast of the course of events. Profoundly religious as he is, he is persuaded that a king (Messiah) is required who shall rule over Israel in the name and spirit of Jehovah, and he is confident that Jehovah will raise one up; his Messianic ideal consists simply in the perfect performance of the ordinary duties of a monarch—there is no reason for thinking that he looks beyond that immediate ideal. In c. xi. his fanciful millennium is simply a hopeful anticipation of the downfall of Assyria (for it was his policy to dissuade an Assyrian alliance) and the rise of a new Davidic kingdom; he has perfect confidence in the ultimate triumph of Jehovah. Thus, also the famous text on the conception by a virgin (vii. 14 sqq.) is now easily understood. The Hebrew word, in the first place, does not mean a "virgin" in the physical sense; it means any young woman of age to become a mother. So far from alluding to the "Virgin" Mary and Christ, Isaiah simply says that any woman who may conceive and bear a child within a year may call him Emmanuel (God with us); foretelling that before the infant reaches the age of intelligent childhood Judah will be laid desolate, all wealth and hindrances to union with God swept away, nothing will be between men and God. It was a political forecast for the coming few years, such as the great statesman often gave; and, like all similar predictions, they were not always realized, and were generally inaccurate in details and exaggerated in colouring.

The most destructive criticism has fallen to the lot of Daniel. Not only is the book not the work of a prophet Daniel of the Babylonian captivity, but the very existence of such an individual is "more than doubtful."* It seems hard to part with the most familiar of the prophets (personally alluded to as the author of the book by Christ), but critics are so unanimous in ascribing the book to the second or third century B.C. that the figure of Daniel recedes into the land of myth. It was compiled by a late Jewish writer out of some old folk-stories. Its date is not quite clear, but, as Driver admits, it cannot be older than 300 B.C., and its date is more probably about 168 or 167, where even Delitzsch puts it. Professor Sayce here conspires with the critics in demolishing the book, pointing out that the writer is entirely unacquainted with Babylonian names and

---

* Reuss, quoted approvingly by Cheyne.

customs. It was the last of a series of forgeries—for forgery it was, as truly as the "Poems of Ossian;" the fact that forgery had become a common practice among Hebrew writers, and was employed by the priestly authorities, does not change its character. And, after supplying Christendom with a dramatic version of the fall of Babylon for 2,000 years, the book is found to be utterly untrustworthy. It is full of grave historical errors. We now know from the cuneiform inscriptions (contradicting Herodotus) that there was no siege of Babylon, and that "the king of the Chaldeans" was *not* slain, as Daniel affirms; that Belshazzar never became king of Babylon at all, and that he was not the son of Nebuchadnezzar, but of Nabonidos; that the successor of Nabonidos was Cyrus (not "Darius the Mede"), and Cyrus was not even a Mede; that Darius was not the son of Ahasuerus, but his father. It is clear that the author is far removed from Babylon and the Babylonian captivity. Hence, Daniel is another extremely incongruous section of an inspired book.

Another very popular prophet who has faded into airy nothingness under the attentions of the critics is Jonah, of balænine notoriety. Dr. Driver gently urges that he "is not strictly historical," whereat Canon Cheyne protests that he is "not in any point" historical. Still, he considerately adds (for the benefit of weaker minds) that "he is not directly mythic," but that the author "used a Babylonio-Israelitish expression of mythic origin." It is commonly admitted that the author (of post-exilic period) invented the incident for didactic purposes, so that the conscience of Christendom is relieved of belief in the famous miracle. Like Tobit and his dog, and Daniel and the lions, Jonah and the whale recede from the stage of serious history. In Zechariah, at chapter ix., a new oracle begins, quite distinct in subject and style, revealing the composite nature of the book. The whole prophecy is unintelligible, unless it is placed a little after the time of Hosea. Nahum is put by Sayce, on archæological grounds, between 666 and 660 B.C. Even the Lamentations are proved not to be the work of Jeremiah. In general, it may be said that the prophets are found to be largely composite and adulterated, and to have a much later date than tradition believed; and, especially, that every so-called prediction finds its sufficient reason in the actual circumstances of the writer. Hence that revolution in the conception of a prophet which has been described, and which is so apparent in the recent work of Dean Farrar and his associates on that subject.*

Such, then, is the series of changes which the higher criticism, literary and historical, has induced in our estimate of the books of Scripture. It is not surprising that an increasing number of Christians are coming to regard the Old Testament as a collection of documents which were not intended for their use ; to whose fate, therefore, Christianity can afford to be indifferent. Many would retain their veneration for it on the ground of its ethical and spiritual value ; but, in that case, it is obviously expedient to make considerable expurgations ; such selected or expurgated editions are, indeed, beginning to appear. As the Bible stands, the grave defects of its contents, its crude and repulsive picture of the deity, and its malodorous details and perverse ideals of conduct, together with the light which modern criticism has thrown upon its composition and historical value, may be thought to outweigh any ethical usefulness it may have for humanity. And when such a selection has been made, it will still be incontestable that the documents will have no higher title to inspiration than the Scriptures of Confucianism, Buddhism, Brahminism, and Zoroastrianism.

Not very many years ago astronomers were startled by the theory that the sun moved rapidly through space. The motion of the stars had been observed, and, the analogy having been extended to our sun, it was found to be drifting rapidly towards Hercules and Lyra. At the present day astronomers have so far recovered from the shock of the discovery that they are prepared to demonstrate *à priori* that the sun *must* move ; that, if their predecessors had only calculated the effect of the law of gravitation upon our system, they would have seen that the sun would have collided with α Centauri ages ago, if it were not on the move ; rapid motion was just what we ought to expect. The change of attitude on the part of Biblical theologians is not unlike that of the astronomers. The critical theory met, at first, with a resistance which only theologians

* "Prophets of the Christian Church," by F. W. Farrar, etc.

can offer. At the present day we are assured that the new character which the Old Testament presents is (like the nebular hypothesis or Darwinism) just what we ought to have expected. Oriental writers were generally anonymous, we are told, and it was quite a familiar practice for them to put the name of some venerated individual at the top of their parchment. If they did not, tradition would almost inevitably do it for them. The great figures of the Old Testament history were men of action, whose entire energy was engrossed in their actual task. It were foolish to expect that they should indite long treatises for the benefit of posterity, and especially that their thoughts should be always centred upon some remote future. So, too, it were unwise to expect the " sense of exactitude " of a Gibbon or a Lecky in Oriental writers many centuries before the Christian era. The Oriental imagination must not be credited with the modern scientific spirit and peculiar interest in exact truth. If we transfer ourselves in thought to the period at which the documents arose and were edited, divesting ourselves of our modern mental habits, we shall recognise that the critical theory of the origin of Scripture contains nothing startling or extraordinary, and may be accepted without scruple. No one will quarrel with theologians for laying this flattering unction to their wounded consciences; but one cannot but notice that it is a complete renunciation of the *doctrine* of inspiration— though not of the *term*—and that it has given an irreparable blow to the teaching authority of the Churches.

The New Testament had been attacked by the older Freethinkers *pari passu* with the Old. Their motive principle was a conviction of the impossibility of miraculous occurrences, hence they were led *à priori* to relegate the whole contents of the Gospels to the region of pious legends. The higher criticism, more exact in research and less ruled by philosophical preconceptions, confined its attention to the Old Testament at the beginning of the century. In 1835 appeared the famous " Leben Jesu " of Strauss, which gave a powerful impetus to New Testament criticism. Strauss's mythic theory is frequently said to be entirely antiquated, and the apologist for the Gospels loves to dwell upon the rise and fall of theories—the mythic, the tendency, the Renanesque, etc., which preceded the actual state of critical opinion. But it can hardly be said that Strauss's theory is entirely extinct. A certain element of it must be retained by all who reject the miraculous legends of the Gospels, and are yet unwilling to consider them forgeries. However, it is true that the interval between the death of Jesus and the appearance of the Gospels is not now thought to have been so great as Strauss imagined, and as the elaborate accretion of myths which he taught would require. To regard the Gospel story as a conglomerate of a few facts and an enormous quantity of innocent fictions like Greek or Roman mythology, or Hindoo theology, we must suppose a longer period of growth than we should, perhaps, be justified in demanding. Still, there was a considerable interval between the events and the publication of their compound narrative. There is actually in that narrative a very large quantity of mythological and superstitious insertions. Hence it is usually thought that, in the interval, the few authenticated facts of Christ's career had been gradually incrusted with the romantic and quasi-mythic additions of unthinking fervour.

However, the school which immediately replaced the mythical school regarded the New Testament documents somewhat in the light of forgeries. No doubt there is much justification for such an hypothesis; literary criticism had discovered a quantity of such forgeries in the Old Testament, ecclesiastics have been convicted of many such during the Christian era (as the Isidorian Decretals and the works of Dionysius the Areopagite), and modern ecclesiastics show an edifying coolness in defending the work of Hilkiah and the priestly writers. The Tübingen school, therefore—a group of Tübingen professors, headed by F. Baur, Zeller, Schwegler, and other Hegelians—rejected the late origin and gradual growth of Strauss, and thought that the books of the New Testament were so many party pamphlets in which facts had been coloured and distorted with partizan zeal, and even direct forgeries admitted. The theory was connected with a larger hypothesis on the origin of the Christian Church. It was thought that two opposing tendencies were discernible in the nascent Church—a conservative, Judaizing, Ebionite tendency and a liberal and latitudinarian tendency under the leadership of Paul; the several parts of the New Testament were discordant emanations of these parties. Thus, in the Apostolic age the Apocalypse sprang from the Ebionite party, the Pauline epistles from their opponents. Of the Gospels, the old Gospel according to the Hebrews (of which Matthew is a later revision) represented the Ebionite faction; Luke and Marcion's Gospel belonged to the Pauline movement. Mark, 2 Peter, and Jude were neutral, and so on. The "tendency theory" led on to a "mediation school," under Hilgenfeld, which admitted the majority of the books to be of the age of the apostles, and considered Paul as the virtual founder of Christianity. The followers of Renan (almost confined to the France which gave him birth) are often called the "romancist school;" the importance, however, of Renan's delineation of the psychological development of Jesus is very great, and the influence of his brilliant "Vie de Jesus" in exciting a critical attitude in unlearned spheres is much too important to be lost sight of. In England, also, in 1874 the appearance of "Supernatural Religion" (which has been previously analyzed) attracted much attention to the criticism of the New Testament.

Though, naturally, less startling than the revelation of the origin of the Old Testament, the results which have been attained in New Testament criticism are of no little importance. The activity of the critics has centred chiefly upon what is called the Synoptic problem. It was early noticed that there was a remarkable similarity between the narratives of the first three Gospels, Mark, Matthew, and Luke; they seem to take a common view of the life of Christ, frequently using even the same language; hence they are called the Synoptic writers. The question how to account for their substantial agreement, with incidental divergencies and even contradictions, gave rise to the Synoptic problem. The problem is now generally solved by assuming that the three writers made use of an earlier document* or documents, a simpler life of Christ, of which they frequently retain the very words. The writers expanded this document at discretion and incorporated independent traditions; as time went on, and they were transcribed and dispersed, other mythical and legendary additions were made, and the

---

* An interesting *résumé* of this common early tradition is found in Mr. F. J. Gould's "Concise History of Religion," vol. iii., p. 117.

actual three gospels were probably in use in the second half of the second century. The actual authorship of the three is, of course, problematical, and is of no importance; a more serious question is that of date, and the evidence is too meagre to afford a precise solution. The Gospel entitled Mark seems to be the earliest, and is usually assigned to the closing period of the first century. The Gospel entitled Matthew, in which critics find traces of composite authorship, is generally referred to the beginning of the second century; as is also the lost Hebrew Gospel of Matthew which St. Jerome mentions. Luke is referred to a more cultured writer of the beginning of the second century.

A keener controversy has arisen over the authorship and character of the Fourth Gospel. In the first half of the present century it is said that, of fifty authorities on the subject, four to one were in favour of the Johannine authorship. Of those who wrote on the subject between 1880 and 1890, two to one were *against* the Johannine authorship.* And, while the majority of orthodox critics have thus surrendered the traditional belief in the Johannine authorship, they have accepted the critical contention that it is historically untrustworthy. "One half of those on the conservative side to-day," says a Christian scholar— "scholars like Weiss, Beyschlag, Sanday, and Reynolds— admit the existence of a dogmatic intent and an ideal element in this Gospel, so that we do not have Jesus's thought in his exact words, but only in substance." It has been characterized by one of the most eminent among recent Christian scholars as "an unhistorical product of abstract reflection."† It represents a mixture of Greek philosophy and Jewish theology, and is probably due to a gifted member of the Alexandrian school during the reign of Hadrian (died 138). It frequently conflicts with the older Gospels, and its historical value is nullified by the ideal tendency of the writer. The Pauline epistles are usually accepted—except the epistle to the Hebrews, whose author is unknown. The first epistle of Peter is also spurious;

---

* *Vide* Crooker, "The New Bible and its Uses."
† *Vide* A. D. White, "Warfare of Science and Theology," vol. ii., p. 385.

the first and second of Timothy and Titus are probably spurious. The Acts are denied to the traditional Luke, and thrown back to about 120–130. The Apocalypse is fundamentally (for it has been much amplified and interpolated) the oldest book of the New Testament, and was probably written in 68 or 69 by an unknown Aramaic writer.

Little interest, however, arises from the discussion of the date, authorship, and integrity of the minor portions of the New Testament. Two issues are made clear by the result of the controversy. The first is that the traditional idea of the origin of the New Testament is entirely inaccurate. A few prominent figures, apostles, and apostolic writers are proposed as the authors by tradition, and each is described as accomplishing his task within a short period of the events he describes, and under a special inspiration. The historical report on their origin is vastly different. Only the epistles of Paul can be definitely traced; the majority have a most precarious origin. During the second century the Christian world was flooded with "inspired" writings, Gospels, Epistles, Revelations, etc., of unknown and irresponsible authorship. The credulity of the early Christians accepted anything and everything that was written of Christ. At length, seeing that heresy was being thus propagated, the Church made a selection from the vast number, and drew up a canon containing the few which we have to-day. The names of prominent apostles were attached to them, but criticism has at length taught us a truer view of their origin.

The second issue has important reference to the dogma of the divinity of Christ. The witness of the prophets to that doctrine had, as we have seen, completely broken down even among orthodox critics. The prophets spoke of, and to, their own times, if we confine our attention to facts. Again, serious trouble arose when it was found that Christ's allusions to the Old Testament were based on a false traditional belief. As Canon Liddon said, in 1889, the authority of Christ, and therefore of Christianity, must rest on the old view of the Old Testament; the old view is utterly untenable to-day. Christ refers psalms to David which he did not write, and the law to Moses. He alluded to Jonah's preaching and adventure with a whale as historical facts. He attributes words to Daniel which were only two hundred years old. He refers to Noah and the Flood, Lot's wife, and other Old Testament myths. There are, of course, many ingenious attempts to explain; but, to one who has no theory to sustain, the natural inference is irresistible, that Christ knew no more of the Old Testament than his audience did. Finally, we now learn that there was a sufficient interval between the death of Christ and the appearance of the Gospels to allow the accretion of all their supernatural stories; that such accretion has followed the lives of Zoroaster, Buddha, Apollonius of Tyana, etc., and would be natural in the present instance; that (as we shall see) many of the supposed supernatural features of Christ's life have a clear pre-Christian origin, and that the writers of the Gospel are unknown Jews of utterly unverifiable authority. Criticism has impartially weighed the external evidence in favour of the credibility of the Gospels, and can find none of sufficient clearness before the writings of Justin in the middle of the second century. Whatever may be said of the genuineness of the Ignatian epistles, etc., the utmost that could be inferred from them would be that there were certain documents in existence in the first century which reappear in the Gospels. The quotations are too slender to allow us to call them witnesses to the existence of the Gospels. We are, therefore, reduced to the fact that the New Testament, as we have it (substantially), was in use in the Churches about the middle of the second century—more than one hundred years after the death of Christ, four generations from the events of his life. In view of that interval, and of the unknown character of the writers, and keeping in sight the analogy of other religions, criticism can only say of the divine features attributed to the Galilean what it says of them in the case of Buddha and Apollonius—"*Fama crescit eundo.*" A few facts about the lives of religious teachers gain enormous accretions of myth and legend in the course of a century or two.

Chapter III.

COMPARATIVE RELIGION AND MYTHOLOGY.

The work of the higher critics in the literary analysis of Scripture is mainly of a destructive character. There is, indeed, a constructive aspect of their activity. Their investigations cast a useful positive light upon the original synthesis and growth of the Christian sacred books. Still, from the point of view of the Rationalist historian, the most interesting result of their labours is the proof that those books contain no indication of a supernatural origin. This negative result is, however, irresistibly confirmed and supplemented by another new science, or rather two new sciences, which the Rationalistic spirit has evoked in the present century—the sciences of comparative religion and comparative mythology. In these sciences the elements themselves which enter into the composition of the Bible are subjected to positive methods of inquiry. The higher criticism was concerned only with the mode of their combination. If these elements, the myths, legends, or doctrines of the Bible, eluded all further scientific analysis, the claim for an extra-rational source would still have a certain *status* as an hypothesis. Before the scientific investigations which we are now going to summarize, such an hypothesis seems to be as hopelessly discredited as the hypothesis of the supernatural formation of the actual books of Scripture. Just as physical science has destroyed the theory of a unique and transcendent interest which antiquity had allotted to our planet among the heavenly bodies, and to the human race amid the many inhabitants of our planet, so also the moral sciences have ruthlessly discredited the old-time theory of a unique character of the Christian religion and literature among the religions and literatures of the world. Like the Greeks and Romans of old, Christians ever regarded all who lay beyond their own frontiers as "barbarians." Towards the beginning of this century the Broad Churchmen, partly from ethical considerations and partly from a shrewd anticipation of the results of the scientific inquiry which had been instituted, evinced a broader and more humane spirit. At the present day impartial science surveys the whole field of religious and sacred books, and fails to perceive other than accidental differences (of degree, not of kind) between them. Here and there a higher pitch of mental development has enabled a race to purify and co-ordinate its traditions more effectively than others have done; but those local modifications present no difficulty to the historian, and in the ultimate analysis the body of myths and legends which have been worked up are traced to a common source, and that source is purely natural.

The two subordinate sciences which minister to the comparative mythologist, and on whose data he ultimately relies, are philology and ethnology—the science of language and that of races. The founding of the science of comparative philology led to a cultivation of the languages in which non-Christian scriptures are written. Their remarkable affinity was at once observed, and, having regard to their greater antiquity, the inference that the Christian Scriptures were founded on them was naturally drawn. For a long time philologists confined themselves to the study of Latin and Greek, and their results, not only in mythology, but in comparative philology itself, were meagre and misleading. Hebrew was set apart as bearing a semi-religious character. Sanscrit, Zend, etc., were contemptuously neglected as the embodiment of presumably grotesque and useless traditions. However, at the beginning of this century Bopp founded the real science of linguistic philology by introducing Sanscrit into the comparison, and pointing out the relation of the Aryan or Indo-European languages. The relation had been glimpsed by our Sir W. Jones in 1786, but had been neglected in England, and, as usual, taken up by German scholars. Bopp's work was developed by J. Grimm and F. A. Pott, and a large number of distinguished scholars, in the first half of the century. In 1866 Schleicher, in his

"Compendium," made an important step in advance by assuming and partially reconstructing a parent speech from which Indians, Persians, and most European nations have derived their languages. Since that time the work of co-ordination has made rapid progress. Ethnology, digesting and analyzing the reports of travellers, and philology, basing its operations on linguistic analysis and comparison, have co-operated in rectifying the vague, erroneous notions which religious tradition had inspired, as it still inspires, in nations who have made no scientific progress. All the nations and races of the world have been arranged in a few great groups, and the affinity of their languages, at least within those groups, has been demonstrated. The old legend of the confusion of tongues has received a death-blow.

Since every race has a religion of some character, a corresponding scheme of religions has been constructed, in which Judaism and Christianity find their natural position. That they are in the front rank of religions every student of the comparative science must admit; that they are foremost in that rank is very disputable, even in the case of Christianity; but that they are entirely outside the ranks no student will claim on scientific grounds. From a comparison of their contents, their myths, and legends (for, since it is the invariable custom of the theologian to call all religious stories myths and legends which differ from his own peculiar dogmata, the non-theological scientist must call *all* religious traditions myths and legends), their genetic affinity with other religions is at once revealed. This family of religions has, naturally, a close resemblance to the ethnological family of races and the philological family of languages; and in all three cases an initial unity, a common proto-parent, is not ambiguously detected: in religion the community of myths all the world over is particularly striking. Thus most of the European religions have been united with those of ancient India, Persia, and Phrygia, under the common title of Aryan religions. In the eastern branch the old Iranian religion was the parent of Magism, Zarathustrianism (or Mazdaism), from which, through the Zendics, were developed Manicheeism (a blending with Christianity) and modern Parsism. The old Indian religion begat Brahmanism, Hinduism, Buddhism, and Jainism; the Phrygian marks a transition between Persian and Greek. The western branch of the Old Aryan religion seems to have given rise to four—Old Pelasgic, Old Wendic, Old German, and Old Celtic; which, in turn, yield the religions of the four great pairs of European races—the Greek-Roman, Letto-Slavic, Norse-Teutonic, and Gaelo-Cymric. The Semitic religions were Old Arabic and Sabæan in the South, from which (blended with Judaism and Christianity) came Mohammedanism, and Babylonian, Assyrian, Hebrew, Canaanitish, Phœnician, Aramaic and Cretan, in the North. Egyptian probably represents a stage of the development of the great Mediterranean race anterior to its separation into Aryan and Semitic. The Confucianism and Taoism of China, the old national religion of Japan, the Finnic religions (of the Mongolians, Turks, Magyars, etc.), form a third great group. All the religions of the world have been classified, and Christianity has shrunk into its due proportions in the great scheme.

The next and the more important task of the student of comparative religion was to trace the unity which pervaded the entire family, and, if possible, reduce their contents to a common source. The task resolves itself into a comparison of the traditional legends of each religion. If the resemblance is found to be very close, the law of probabilities bids us infer a community of origin, or an interchange, as circumstances may direct. Here it is that comparative mythology has come into conflict with traditional Christianity, and the result has been another decisive victory of the Rationalistic spirit. Light has poured in from every quarter of the globe. The Chinese Y-king have been sedulously studied, the Hindoo Vedas are almost as familiar to scholars as the Bible, the Zend-Avesta are widely read, the key to the hieroglyphic writings of Egypt (whose "Book of the Dead" is the oldest scripture known) and of Mexico has been found, the cuneiform writings of Babylonia and Assyria have been deciphered, the sacred songs of the most obscure races have been translated, and travellers have brought us the myths of the most distant races. Upon these data many generations of scholars have laboured—Benfey, Pott, Kuhn, Mannhardt, Grossmann, Breal, Darmesteter, Osthoff, Roscher, Mehlis, Meyer, Decharme, Victor Henry, Barth, V. Schroeder, Bloomfield, Hopkins, Fay, etc., and they have agreed upon the substantial unity of elements in the great variety of religions, and will admit no exception to the law of natural development.

Here, again, there is a profession of opposition to the great body of mythologists, so ably represented in England by Professor Max Müller. Mr. Lang, a competent critic and well-informed mythologist, though neither a philologist like Max Müller, nor an anthropologist like Tylor, heads the revolt against the Rationalist school. But there is here a similar confusion to that which we have seen in the preceding chapter. There is no more opposition between ethnological mythology and philological than there is between the literary criticism of the Bible and Assyriology. The Rationalists have, for the present, confined their attention principally to the Aryan religions. Mr. Lang adduces non-Aryan myths, to which, he thinks, their explanations cannot be extended. The positions of Lang and Max Müller are simply those of Cheyne and Sayce on the critical question. Like the dispute about the mode of the ultimate origin of myths, such controversy tends only to obscure the results which are already established, and withdraw attention from their profound significance. In one word, all the supposed distinctive doctrines of Christianity have been traced to earlier religions; there is no element of direct revelation either in Judaism or in Christianity. In proof of that thesis, and before proceeding to the further conclusion of the mythologists, it is well to summarize some of the evidence which has been collected. That the scientific form which Christian dogmas have in the more elaborate theologies (of the Roman, Anglican, and Greek Churches) is a natural development no one will question. The process by which they have been constructed out of the simpler statements of the Gospels is made clear by the labours of such scholars as Neander and Harnack. But, if we take the simple version of Christian doctrine, which is common to all Christian sects (not, of course, including Unitarianism under that title), and which is clearly contained in the Bible, we shall find, on comparison with the legends of older religions all over the world, that it was no new revelation, but a modification of old myths, which can be ultimately traced to a natural origin. We commence with the Christology of the New

Testament, the story of the birth, life, and death of Christ, which was thought the most distinctive element of the new religion, and the clear embodiment of a divine manifestation at the commencement of the Christian era. It is now clear that that story was borrowed from other religions and adapted to the life of Christ during the long interval which elapsed between his death and the appearance of the Gospels. Even minute details of the legend are found in many earlier religions with which later Judaism came in contact.

The Vedic hymns of the Hindoo religion contain a clear prototype of the life of Christ. Their date is disputed; Max Müller puts it at 1200 B.C., others much earlier. Vishnu (the legend runs), the second person of the Trinity, being moved at the sight of the sin and misery of the earth, became incarnate under the name of Chrishna. He was born of the virgin Devaki on the 25th of December. His birth was announced by a star, and accompanied by the singing of a chorus of Devatas (spirits). Although he was of royal descent, even by his human parentage, he was born in a cave, his mother being on a journey with his foster-father to pay tribute to the king. The cave was brilliantly illuminated, and the divine child was recognised by cowherds, who prostrated themselves and offered him perfumes. He was also visited by a holy prophet. The reigning monarch, King Kansa, sought his life, but his foster-father was warned by a heavenly voice to fly with the child. Representations of the flight are found in most of the ancient Hindoo temples. The king thereupon ordered a massacre of all the male infants born on the night of Chrishna's birth. This was represented by an immense sculpture on the roof of the temple of Elephanta many centuries before the birth of Christ. Chrishna astonished his teachers by his precocious wisdom, and, in later life, healed lepers, the deaf, the blind, etc., and raised the dead to life. He had twelve favourite disciples. A woman once poured a vessel of ointment over his head. He was in constant strife with the Evil One. He was chaste, humble, etc., and even washed the feet of the Brahmans. He was transfigured before his beloved disciple Arjuna. Finally he met his death by crucifixion. He is represented in the temples with his arms extended, hanging on a cross, with nailmarks in his hands and feet, and a spear-wound in his side. At his death the sun was darkened, and myriads of demons and spirits were found everywhere. He descended into hell, rose from the dead the third day, and ascended bodily into heaven. It is believed that he will come again in the last days to judge the dead, when the sun and moon will be darkened, and the stars will fall from the firmament. His mother, Devaki, is also called Aditi, which, in the Rig-Veda, is a name for the dawn. Indra, who is worshipped in some parts of India as a crucified god, is represented in the Vedic hymns as son of Dahana (= Daphne), a personification of the dawn. The worship of Chrishna was practised in India at the time of the invasion of Alexander the Great. Chrishna seems to have been deified about the fourth century B.C., but the general outlines of his history were accepted about 900 B.C. He was known by all the titles which were afterwards given to Christ—Saviour, Redeemer, Mediator, the Resurrection and the Life, Lord of Lords, the Great God, the Holy One, and the Good Shepherd.

A few centuries later in Indian religious history we have another signal prototype of Christ. The legend of Chrishna is applied to an historical personage. Siddartha Gautama, or the Buddha (Enlightened One), was born in the fifth century B.C., through the agency of the Holy Spirit, after the visit of a heavenly messenger to his virgin mother, Maha-Maya. An angelic chorus announced at his birth that there was born "a saviour unto all nations of the earth." His birth was reported to the king as a menace to his own position; he was presented in the temple; he was lost by his guardians, and found astonishing the *rishis* (sages) with his discourses; he had a long fast and prayer in the desert, was tempted, and put the tempter to flight by quoting the Veda, received the ministry of angels, and took a bath in the river, when the heavens were opened above him; he had frequent interviews with two Buddhas who had preceded him. One of his disciples was often called the Pillar of Faith, another the Bosom Friend; a third was a Judas, who attempted to destroy his master, and met with a disgraceful death. He walked on the Ganges, healed the sick, and had miraculous escapes from his foes; he was always poor, though of royal descent, and he instructed his disciples to travel without money. His disciples received the power of healing, of expelling demons, and of speaking tongues, and some of them were delivered from prison by an angel. About the end of his life Buddha was transfigured on Mount Pandana, in Ceylon. At his death, at which faithful women were present, the earth trembled, the rocks were split, and spirits appeared; he descended into hell; the lid of his coffin was supernaturally opened and the grave-clothes unwound, and he ascended bodily into heaven. Tradition gave him the titles of Lion of the tribe of Sakya, Only-begotten, the Word, the Way, Truth, and Life, Prince of Peace, Good Shepherd, Light of the World, the Christ (or Anointed) or Messiah, the Saviour of the World. His mother Maya was believed to have been assumed bodily into heaven.

Such were the legends treasured in India centuries before the time of Christ, and with which Judæa became familiar about that period. That the Christology of the New Testament was derived from them cannot be reasonably doubted. If the relative chronological positions of Buddhism and Christianity were reversed, the solution of the problem would be felt to be easy indeed. But the same legend is found in nearly every religion, and from some of them other details of Christian doctrine and practice have been borrowed.

The Mithrians of Persia had a similar version of the story. The Only-begotten Son of God came down from heaven to be a mediator between God and man, and to save men from their sins. He was born on December 25th, when his nativity is annually celebrated with great rejoicing. He was visited by magi, who offered him gold, frankincense, and myrrh. He was called the Logos, the Christ or the Anointed, and the Lamb of God. The ejaculation which is common in Catholic prayers, "Lamb of God who taketh away the sins of the world, have mercy on us, give us peace," is taken from the litanies which the Persian priests sang in honour of Mithras. He was put to death, remained three days in hell, then rose again from the dead. His resurrection was annually celebrated at midnight on March 24th. Egypt had two remarkable versions of the legend. Osiris (a name of the sun) was an incarnation of the second person of the Trinity, called the Word. He was born on December 25th of the virgin Neith or Nut (the Lady of the Sycamore). At his birth a voice proclaimed: "The ruler of all the earth is born." He conquered many temptations, but was finally overcome by his enemies. His sufferings and death were commemorated annually in the early spring, when the mourning song was followed in three days by the language of triumph and the illumination of his tomb. The "Book of the Dead" represents him as the Judge of the dead, as "seeing all things and hearing all things;" and in the most ancient monuments he is represented as carrying the *crux ansata*. His symbol was a serpent (which was the earliest symbol of the Nazarene), and his monogram was the solar wheel or Chrism, in Greek letters a compound of χ and ρ, which has been since appropriated to Christ, and is often found on Roman Catholic vestments. He was called the Lord of Life, the Resurrected One, the Eternal Ruler, the Father of Goodness and Truth. His mother Neith was worshipped as the Immaculate Virgin; the Feast of Lamps, which was held in February in her honour, has become the Candlemas Day of the Christian world. The second Saviour of the Egyptians was Horus (another name of the sun), who was born of the Immaculate Virgin Isis (the moon), in a temple where the sacred cow and bull were kept, on December 25th; on that day his image was annually exhibited in a manger, amid great rejoicing. Horus was of royal descent, and his life was sought by Typhon (darkness, or night); he met many temptations, performed many miracles, was slain, descended into hell, rose on the third day, and ascended into heaven. His death and resurrection were annually celebrated with great pomp. He was called the Royal Good Shepherd, the Only-begotten, the Saviour, the Anointed (or Christ), and the Redeemer. He is generally represented as sitting in the lap of Isis, and both are sometimes black. Since many of the most ancient pictures and statues in Italy of the Virgin and Child are black, it is most probable that they are ancient images of Isis and Horus (in some cases of Devaki and Chrishna—the Hindoo virgin and child). Many pictures now worshipped as representing the Holy Family are certainly pictures of Isis and Horus—the inscription "Deo Soli" betrays their pagan origin. Isis was worshipped, even in Europe, centuries before and after the Christian era, and was called the Virgin-mother, Our Lady, Queen of Heaven, Star of the Sea, Mother of God, Intercessor. She was represented as standing on the crescent moon, and having twelve stars round her head; pilgrimages were made to her temples, and miracles performed at them—in a word, nearly all the details of the Catholic worship of the virgin are taken from the cult of Isis.

Greece had many saviours born of illicit intercourse of gods with virgins. Hercules was a favourite of the Greeks, though he had been worshipped independently in Ethiopia, Egypt, Scythia, Africa, Germany, Spain, the Indies, etc. According to the Greek legend, he was born of Zeus and Alcmene on the 25th of December, when Zeus announced from heaven that he was to be the "mightiest of men." He was swallowed by a fish, in which he remained three days and three nights (like Jonah and Christ); he ascended into heaven in a cloud from his funeral pile. At his death there was darkness on the face of the earth, and thunder came from heaven; the virgin Iola (dawn) was present, whom he speaks of having seen and loved "in the morning-time." There is a close parallel between his famous labours and the signs of the zodiac. He was called the Saviour, the Only-begotten, the Universal Word, the Generator, the Ruler of all things. Dionysius (or Bacchus) is another god from whom both Moses and Christ (or their apotheosizers) have borrowed. He was born of Zeus and the virgin Semele on the 25th of December; by order of Cadmus (Semele's father, whom it was predicted that he should overthrow) he was cast into the Nile, but rescued; he worked miracles, changed water into wine, and his rod into a serpent; crossed the Red Sea at the head of his army, and drew water from the rock. He was represented as horned, and called the Law-giver, also the Slain One, Sin-bearer, Only-begotten Son, Saviour, and Redeemer. His death and resurrection were annually celebrated in early spring. The monogram, I.H.S., which is vulgarly read " I have suffered," and clerically translated " Jesus Hominum Salvator," or as the first three letters of the Greek name Jesus, is the monogram of Bacchus, which has been transferred to Jesus. One of Christ's miracles comes directly from him; he was the god of the vine, and to commemorate his changing of the water of the soil into wine (vine-juice) at his annual festival at Elis, three flagons of water were locked up all night and found changed into wine in the morning—by a sacerdotal process which is elucidated in the fragment *Bel and the Dragon*. Perseus was another Saviour, who was born of Jupiter and the virgin Danae in a shower of gold. The goddess Cybele was another virgin-mother who was honoured as Mother of God and Queen of Heaven. Lady-day was originally a feast of Cybele, and many of her hymns are now sung in Italy in honour of the "virgin" Mary.

Scandinavia had a Saviour, the son of Odin or Woden (heaven) and a virgin goddess Frigga; he was pierced by the sharp thorn of winter, descended into hell, and rose again to life and immortality. The ancient Germans worshipped a virgin-mother and child; the mother's name was Ostâra or Eostre, from which comes our Easter—centuries before the Christian era this feast was preceded by a fast of forty days, initiated by a Carne-Vale (farewell to meat). The ancient Chinese had also the idea of redemption through the sufferings and death of a divine Saviour—Tien, the Holy One, who was "one with God" before anything was made. Lao-Tse (born 604 B.C.) was also believed by them to be the incarnation of a divine emanation who descended upon earth, and was born of a virgin. The Chinese worshipped the Shin-moo (holy mother—a virgin) from time immemorial, representing her, as Christians do, with rays round her head and burning tapers before her images.

A virgin-born god and saviour is found in all the ancient religions of America. In Mexico the saviour, Quetzalcoatle, was the son of Texcatlipoca (the supreme god) and the virgin Sochiquetzal (worshipped as virgin-mother and queen of heaven). His birth was preceded by an angelic annunciation and heralded by a star; he was tempted by the Devil; his disciples observed a forty days' fast. He was crucified for the sins of mankind. The sun was darkened at his death; he descended into hell and rose from the dead. His death and resurrection were celebrated annually in the early spring, when victims were nailed to a cross and shot with an arrow. The Mexicans looked for his second advent, and, indeed, mistook Cortez, the invader, for him. The Mayas of Yucatan, and the Muyscas of Colombia and Nicaragua, had a virgin-born god. According to the Peruvians, the sun (their god) sent his son, Manco Capac, to instruct men in religion; so also taught the Edues of the Californians. In Brazil there was Zoma, like the Quetzalcoatle of Mexico; and the Iroquois and Algonquins had an incarnate-god teacher.

The Assyrians and Babylonians had a virgin mother and child; the mother was Mylitta, and the son Tammuz, or Adonis (the Adonai of Scripture), the Saviour and Mediator. He was born on December 25th, suffered, and was slain (one account says crucified). He descended into hell, rose on the third day, and ascended into heaven. His death and resurrection were celebrated in early spring, with rites similar to those of the Church of Rome. His image (in which a large wound appeared in the side) was laid on a bier and bewailed, and afterwards carried to the tomb with great solemnity.

Another dogma closely connected with that of Redemption, and which Christianity has similarly borrowed from older religions, is the doctrine of the Fall of Man. Among the most ancient traditions of the Hindoos is one of the Tree of Life guarded by spirits in a Paradise watered by four rivers. Another tradition runs that Siva, as God, wishing to tempt Brahma (who had taken human form), dropped from heaven a blossom of the sacred fig-tree. Swayambhura (the incarnate), instigated by his wife Satarupa, obtains it, thinking to become immortal and divine. He is then cursed by Siva, and doomed to misery and degradation. The sacred fig-tree is regarded by the Brahmanists and Buddhists as the Tree of Knowledge. The Hindoos have also the legend of the Deluge and of Babel. The Persians had a legend of the fall of the first parents who were tempted by the evil one in the form of a serpent. The legend is like the Christian one in all particulars. It speaks of Eiren (Eden) as the original abode of man, of the River of Life, the Deluge, the war in heaven, the Millennium, the Jonah incident. The Egyptians had the myth of the tree of life, and of the war in heaven. The Greek legend of the Garden of the Hesperides, in which there was a tree bearing golden apples of immortality, guarded by three nymphs and a dragon, is well known. The Scandinavians had stories of Eden and the Golden Age, and of the Deluge (from which only one man escaped in an ark with his family). The Chinese had a legend of a Golden Age, and a "delicious" garden, surrounded by four rivers, in which were apples of immortality, guarded by a dragon. Almost, in the words of the Old Testament, or of "Paradise Lost," the Chi-King says: "Our misery did not come from heaven, but from a woman." They had also legends of the Deluge and the Millennium. The Mexicans baptized their infants (as did the Brahmanists, Mithrians, etc.) to wash away the sin that tainted the child before the foundation of the world. In their representations the first woman was always accompanied by a serpent, and she was said to have lost Paradise by plucking roses called the "Fruit of the Tree." Their Deluge and Babel legends are remarkably like the Hebrew. Indeed, the Hebrew legends of Genesis have been directly traced to Babylonian sources.*

The Trinity is another dogma which has been borrowed by the early Christians and adapted to Christ's terminology of Father, Son, and Holy Spirit. In the Hindoo trinity Brahma was the father, Vishnu the son, and Siva the destroyer, though, in course of time, the character of the latter was modified, and came to be symbolized by a dove. The Buddhists worship one god in trinity. The Egyptian Osiris, the second person, or Logos, was represented with a trefoil on his head. When Thulis appealed to Serapis, the god replied: "First God, afterward the Word, and with them the Holy Spirit." The Scandinavians had a triune god, so had the Phœnicians, Assyrians, Babylonians, Peruvians, Mexicans, and Chinese.

The sacraments of the Christian Church, Baptism and the Eucharist, are also derived from more ancient religions. Baptism was a feature of the water-cult which was practised throughout the entire Pagan world. The ceremony was performed, sometimes both by immersion and aspersion, and generally accompanied by the sign of the cross, and by the imposition of a name, by the Hindoos, Buddhists, Persians, Egyptians, Scandinavians, Mexicans, and many others. Even the rite of circumcision was not confined to the Hebrews, but practised in Egypt, Ethiopia, Arabia, Phœnicia, and Syria. The Eucharist is an interesting

---

* "The Higher Criticism and the Verdict of the Monuments," by Professor Sayce.

survival of the old nature-religions. Transubstantiation is one of the most ancient of doctrines, and is merely a symbol of the change of soil into human food (wheat). The Greeks celebrated the Eleusinian mysteries every five years in honour of Ceres (the Goddess of Corn, who was said to "have given them her flesh to eat") and Bacchus (the god of wine, who had "given them his blood to drink"). This was probably the immediate source of the Christian Eucharist. In ancient Egypt the sacred cake was consecrated by the priest just as it is to-day by Roman priests. He made the sign of the cross over it, and it became "flesh of his flesh." The Mexican priests consecrated cakes of cornmeal mixed with blood, and gave it to the people as the "flesh of the Saviour." (Their priests had also reached the advanced stage of auricular confession and absolution.) The Assyrians and Babylonians had the sacrament of bread and wine.

So, also, the principal symbols, ceremonies, and festivals of Christianity are borrowed from Paganism. The sacred symbols of the Brahmanists were the cross, serpent, dove, mitre, crosier, key, fish, and sacred heart—all of which were assumed by the Christians. The Buddhists of Tartary have œcumenical councils, monasteries, nunneries, pulpits, dalmatics, bell-ringing, incense, thuribles, chalices, rosaries, chanted services, litanies, aspersions with holy water, priests with shaven polls, prayers for the sick, baptism, eucharist, auricular confession, extreme unction, masses for the dead, worship of relics, weekly and yearly festivals, feasts of the Immaculate Conception and Candlemas, worship of one god in trinity, and belief in heaven, hell, and purgatory. Buddhism (in existence for more than 2,400 years) is the established religion of Burmah, Siam, Laos, Cambodia, Thibet, Japan, Tartary, Ceylon, and Loochoo, besides counting two-thirds of China and a large portion of Siberia. It has more than four hundred million adherents. Hinduism and Buddhism together embrace more than half the world. In ancient Egypt there was great splendour of ritual. The priests were shaven and shorn, and wore white surplices and gorgeous robes, mitres, tiaras; wax-tapers, processions, lustrations of holy water, signs of the cross, sacraments, etc., were familiar in their rites. From Scandinavia comes the curious old custom of eating boar at Christmas. A Scandinavian god, Freya, was fabled to have been killed by a boar at the Winter Solstice; hence the Scandinavians offered a boar annually at the Feast of Yule. In China, Easter was celebrated annually with much pomp as a feast of gratitude to Tien. The cross, which has so long been regarded as the peculiar symbol of Christianity, was venerated from time immemorial throughout the Pagan world. Centuries before it became an ornament on the chaste bosoms of Christian maidens, it had been pressed with more intense but less holy fervour to the bosoms of Egyptian and other maidens; for, in many cases at least, it was certainly a phallic symbol. It was venerated throughout Egypt, Persia, Babylonia, India, Japan, Thibet, America, etc. It was placed on the figures of the gods, on coins and seals, and worn as an ornament; and temples were often built in the form of a cross.

From these data Rationalism has been enabled to supplement the negative conclusions of the higher critics with important positive and constructive theories. It is clear from this accumulated evidence of philology, history, archæology, and ethnology that the doctrines so curiously woven into the fabric of the Bible came from anterior human traditions, and not from a special revelation vouchsafed to the Hebrew or the Christian writers. Given a communication, or even a probability of a communication, nothing could be more unscientific than to postulate a different version of the origin of the legends. It may be well to indicate some of the evidence which Rationalistic science adduces in favour of such communication.

It is a common practice of theologians to enlarge upon the aptness of the time and place chosen for the birth of Christianity. Judea had become the high-road between all the great nations of antiquity. It lay between Ethiopia, Egypt, Libya, Asia Minor, Greece, and Rome on one side, and India, Syria, Arabia, Persia, Assyria, and Babylonia on the other. In this lay its peculiar power of assimilating alien religious traditions. It had been visited successively by Egyptians, Assyrians, Persians, Greeks, and Romans, and some elements from each had infiltrated into the old Canaanitish religion. Indeed, that the Old Testament is a collection of alien traditions is beyond dispute. The projected analysis of its contents by the *anti-critical* school will complete the work. The point which Rationalistic writers have principally sought to establish is the connection of Buddhism with Christianity and the growth of the New Testament from Pagan myths which were adapted to Christ as they had been adapted to Buddha and Confucius. The mere comparison of Christian rites and doctrines (in the unorganized condition) with those of Buddhism fully justifies the Rationalist assumption; still, abundant evidence of their connection is forthcoming.

About 250 B.C. a royal convert to Buddhism, Asoka, was seized with the proselytizing mania, and indulged it with royal bounty. He scattered 80,000 missionaries throughout the known world—through India, China, Japan, Ceylon, Persia, Babylonia, Syria, Palestine, and Egypt. A passage in his edicts, engraven on a rock at Girnur in Guzerat, shows that Buddhism was planted in the dominion of the Seleucidæ and Ptolemies in the third century B.C. The Buddhistic teaching, which had been accepted by large numbers of Jews (retaining the Mosaic Law), comes down to the time of Christ in the sect of the Essenes. Three salient points in the teaching of the Essenes—asceticism, celibacy, and voluntary poverty—are entirely antagonistic to the Hebrew system, and are just as conspicuously Buddhistic. These doctrines are precisely the characteristic features of the teaching of Christ; his individuality only shows itself in his warm sympathy with the wretched and sinful. Of the four Jewish sects of his time Christ denounces three vigorously on all occasions—the Scribes, Pharisees, and Sadducees—and never says a word against the Essenes. There is every reason to think that Christ was a member of that sect, and that the distinctive features of his preaching were Essenic, and thus, indirectly, Buddhistic. But the chief influence of Buddhism is apparent in the growth of Christ-legends during the century which followed his death. We have seen that the life of Christ was not committed to documents during the first century, and thus the mythopœic faculty had a license which it is difficult to appreciate in modern times. Gautama had foretold the coming of another angel-messiah in about 600 years: the Galilean must be he. Alexandria had been reached by Asoka's missionaries, and it was there that an exuberant growth of Christian literature appeared, which was arbitrarily divided into inspired and uninspired. But in both apocryphal and canonical works the stories that are told of the obscure Galilean, whom the eye of the historian can scarcely reach, are clearly borrowed from Buddhistic, Greek, and Egyptian legends. This connection of Christianity with "paganism" through the Essenes is not entirely a modern discovery.

Philo* maintains the identity in creed of higher Judaism and the "Gymnosophists" of India. Eusebius and Epiphanius identify the Essenes with the early Christians. Ammonius Saccus, founder of the Neo-Platonic school, said that Christianity and Paganism differed in nothing essential, and had a common origin. Celsus said that "the Christian religion contains nothing but what Christians hold in common with heathen—nothing new." Many of the fathers admit that Christian teaching was not new, and that many concessions were made to Paganism. Gregory of Naz., writing to S. Jerome, says: "A little jargon is all that is necessary to impose on the people. The less they comprehend, the more they admire. Our forefathers and doctors have often said, not what they thought, but what circumstances and necessity dictated." Eusebius, as Gibbon says, "indirectly confesses that he has related what might redound to the glory, and that he has suppressed all that could tend to the disgrace, of religion." Minucius Felix, in his Octavius, puts these words in the mouth of Cecilius: "All these fragments of crack-brained opiniatry and silly solaces played off in the sweetness of song by deceitful [Pagan] poets, by you too credulous creatures [the Christians], have been shamefully reformed and made over to your own God." Faustus makes the same accusation to St. Augustine. The learned Christian advocate, M. Turretin, says (of the fourth century): "It was not so much the Pagans who were converted to Christianity, but Christianity was converted to Paganism." Hadrian could not see the difference between Christians and the worshippers of the ancient Egyptian god Serapis (a sungod). King says that the worship of Serapis was incor-

---

* See S. Titcombe's "Aryan Sun Myths" for a large number of authorities

porated with Christianity in the East, and that all the early portraits of Christ were clearly taken from the head of Serapis; the early Christians were often called sun-worshippers. Christ was not represented in art as a man on a cross until the seventh century; he was represented as the Good Shepherd—a figure borrowed from Apollo, Mercury, and other gods, and a title common in all religions. He was also represented as a Lamb; this is also a pagan myth. The sign Aries (the Ram) was formerly a Lamb, and the worship of Aries in ancient religions was equivalent to the worship of the sun passing through Aries. Aries was called the Saviour—"the Lamb of God which taketh away the sins of the world," in words which the Catholic Church now applies to Christ daily. On an ancient Phœnician medal there is a "Lamb of God" with cross and rosary.

The last point brings us to the consideration of the further problem of the mythologist—the connection of myths with a primitive nature worship. Those who desire to cling to the idea of a supernatural revelation might imagine the legends which enter into the composition of the Bible to be revealed in the first instance. Such a belief is excluded by the labours of mythologists. All myths have not yet been explained, but the majority and the most important are satisfactorily explained. "The question whether most of the ancient gods and heroes derived their origin from physical phenomena has been answered once for all by the Veda, and I do not know of a single scholar who, if able to read the Veda, would express any doubt on this subject;"[*] and again: "That the gods were originally personified representatives of the most prominent phenomena of nature, nearly all serious students of mythology agree." There are, of course, controversies as to the manner in which the descriptions passed into personal legends, but this does not weaken the substantial agreement of mythologists of their naturalistic origin. So far, then, from these stories, which advanced religions have elaborated into a dogmatic scheme, coming from a supernatural revelation, they are merely idealized versions of astronomical and other

---

[*] Professor Max Müller, "Contributions to the Science of Mythology."

physical phenomena as they appeared to the primitive mind. In particular, the Christology which is found in every organized religion is a mythicized representation of the sun's relation to the earth which has expanded in the lapse of time, and has been adapted to innumerable personalities, and last of all to Jesus of Nazareth ; neither are the more ancient Christ-stories predictions of future events, nor is the Christian soteriology the description of an historical episode—all alike are manipulations of a solar myth whose origin had been lost sight of.

It is in the Vedic hymns, as Max Müller says, that we find the development of the sun into a god—a Creator, Preserver, Ruler, Rewarder, and Saviour. The Vedas take us nearest of all to the religion of our Aryan ancestors, and there are passages which explicitly indicate the solar nature of the Redeemer. " Let us worship again the Child of Heaven, the Son of Strength, Arusha, the Bright Light of the Sacrifice. He rises as a mighty flame, he stretches out his wide arms, he is ever like the wind. His light is powerful, and his mother—the Dawn—gives him the best share of worship among men ;" and in the Rig-Veda he is spoken of as " stretching out his arms in the heavens to bless the world, and to rescue it from the terror of darkness." Indeed, from the Aryan name for the supreme being, Dyaus, which has passed into most of the Aryan languages (Theos, deus, dio, etc.), the astronomical nature of the primitive deity is sufficiently apparent : it comes from a root which meant "to shine," and was applied to the bright sky overhead, which was man's first god. The sun was then worshipped as his son, born of the earth, or the darkness, or the dawn, etc., and sent by him to break the power of darkness, to redeem mankind from the misery of night and of winter ; the earth was also worshipped as the universal mother.

In support of this theory of the solar nature of the Christs or Saviours of all nations, there is an overwhelming mass of evidence. In the first place, the very names of the Christ and his mother point to an astronomical origin. Aditi and Dahana, the Hindoo virgin-mothers, are names of the dawn. Osiris was a name of the sun ; Isis, mother of Horus, was the moon. Theseus was born of Aithra (the pure air), Œdipus of Iokasté (violet light of the morning), Hercules of Io (violet-tinted dawn), the Scandinavian Christ of Woden (heaven), and so on in the Zettish songs and old Greek myths, and in the religions of Egypt, Babylon, Mexico, Peru, and Central America. "With scarcely an exception," says Cox, "all the names by which the virgin-goddess was known point to the mythology of the dawn." The 25th of December, which is universally celebrated as the Saviour's birthday, is precisely the commencement of the sun's northward journey after the winter solstice; at that time the constellation Virgo is rising in the Eastern horizon—hence the immaculate virgin of all the Christ legends. In the first decan of the Virgin in the Persian sphere an immaculate virgin is represented; "she nourishes," says Abulmazar, "and suckles a babe which some [nations] call Jesus, and the Greeks call Christ." The inscription of the virgin-goddess of Sais reads: "The fruit which I have brought forth is the sun;" she was delivered about the winter solstice, according to Plutarch. The virgin in the Indian zodiac has a lotus (lily) in her hand; in the Egyptian zodiacs she nurses the child Horus; in one old zodiac she is represented as a virgin nursing a child, seated on clouds, and having a star on her head. The transition from the constellation Virgo presiding at the winter birth of the sun to Maia, Maya, or Maria—the virgin-mother of Hermes, Buddha, and Jesus—is obvious; the whole Mariology of the Catholic Church is borrowed from astronomy, and is only really applicable to the constellation Virgo.

Again, in the star which heralds the birth of the Saviour in all mythologies (and which modern commentators of the New Testament so ingeniously explain on principles of modern astronomy) we must recognise the planet Venus, the "morning star" which heralds the daily birth of the sun. Nearly all the Saviours are born in a cave or dungeon—this is the dark abode from which the sun emerges every morning. It is predicted that he will destroy the ruling monarch—*i.e.*, dispel the darkness of night, and the monarch (*e.g.*, the Egyptian Typhon [darkness]) seeks his life. All the Saviours, or sun-gods, leave their homes and mothers to benefit mankind—the sun rising in the heavens to shine upon men; they meet with many foes (clouds of storm and darkness), but always prevail; they travel over many lands with their twelve companions (the twelve signs of the zodiac on which are modelled the labours of Hercules and the life of Buddha), ever toiling for others and doing good; they meet with an early and violent death (the end of summer), and are generally crucified in the heavens, slain or pierced with the spear (thorn or arrow) of winter. At the Saviour's death his disciples desert him, but his mother (the dawn or dusk) re-appears, and finally a darkness overspreads the land, and the Saviour descends into Hell or Hades; Hades in olden times was not a place of torment, but the place of all the departed, and was located by the Aryans in the Far West. He rises from Hades after three days; on the 22nd of December the sun appears to remain in the same place for three days and three nights, and then commences his ascent into the heavens. As the sun rises above the equator at the Vernal Equinox, this resurrection of the sun was generally celebrated on the 25th of March. The fish, the lamb, the cross, and the serpent were widely consecrated to the sun—and to the Saviours. The sign Aries was formerly called the Lamb, and when the sun made the transit of the equinox under this sign it was called the Lamb of God; hence the name of Mithras, and Jesus, and many other sun-gods. The serpent, which brings ruin to mankind, seems to be the constellation of that name which ushers winter into the world, and over which the sun finally prevails. In fact, almost every detail of the Saviour-legend which is the life and soul of Christian doctrine points to the solar origin of the myth: the nature of his functions, the time and manner of his birth and death, the very terminology of the story in older literature, is transparently astronomical. Looking back on the myths which we have summarized above, we see that they only find an adequate explanation in the solar theory. The Great Father of all modern religions is but a transformed conception of the broad vault of heaven that shone on our child-like ancestors: his son, the Redeemer, is the beneficent luminary that brings light and hope and joy to humanity after the darkness of night and misery of the winter. History repeats itself: at this end of the nineteenth century science proclaims that the one supreme source of all life, energy, and motion on the surface of our planet is its genial and inspiring luminary.

It is a long journey from the primitive nature-worship to the ethical monotheism of Isaiah, Plato, and Christ, and the students of comparative religion are far from unanimous in retracing it. Indeed, there is a discussion as to the manner in which the early myths passed from their original meaning into accounts of legendary gods and heroes. Mr. Spencer thinks the stories first related to incidents in the lives of actual ordinary individuals, but the vast majority of mythologists agree with Max Müller that they were transferred directly from natural phenomena (their application to which was lost sight of) to historical personages; Professor Max Müller thinks the process due to a "disease of language"—the later Aryans found the solar terms in their languages, were ignorant of their true application, and founded the legends upon them. However that may be, the earliest stage of religion to which science can attain is a kind of chaotic, indistinct naturism; the primitive man, in the first faint glimmer of reflection, falls awe-stricken before the more impressive phenomena of nature which he considers as the acts of living powers; he has no consciousness of personality, or spirituality, or of his superiority over the animals, hence his gods are mere undefined powers. The life about him gradually takes shape, and there arises a number of polydœmonistic religions with much magic and sorcery; in some quarters a decadence into fetishism. To this succeeds a definite polytheism, in some cases therianthropic, in others anthropomorphic, which in many tribes becomes a henotheism—a recognition of one supreme god with many others, a national or relative and practical (not speculative) monotheism. Many of the nature myths are already legendary, and sometimes the vague oral tradition is embodied in sacred books or laws, thus giving rise to nomistic or nomothetic religions, in China, India, Persia, etc. Anthropomorphic polytheism is gradually subdued by pantheism or by monotheism, and national religions are overcome by universal or world religions of a proselytizing disposition, such as Buddhism, Christianity, and Mohammedanism. Ethical religions are the final development, such as Confucianism, Brahmanism, Jainism, Mazdaism, and Judaism (non-proselytic), and Buddhism and Christianity (proselytic). Through such a process has been developed the ethical monotheism which the course of political events during the last 1700 years has imposed upon the acceptance of Europe. How Rationalistic criticism has disposed of its claims to be a positive supernatural revelation we have seen in this and the preceding chapter; the following chapter will describe the effect of Rationalistic progress upon the philosophical systems with which it has been buttressed by those who felt the weakness of its historical foundation.

Chapter IV.

RATIONALISM AND PHILOSOPHY.

Mr. Lecky says in his History, concerning "the habit of thought which is the supreme arbiter of the opinions of successive ages," that "those who have contributed most largely to its formation are, I believe, the philosophers." Philosophers, as a rule, dwell in heights that are inaccessible to the great multitude; their systems and conclusions are the most difficult of all sciences to popularize. Yet it is true that the philosophic systems that prevail in the academies of each successive age exercise a profound influence upon the whole thought of their generation. They impart a tone and give a point of view to the large army of popular writers, of poets, historians, scientists, etc., who mediate between the multitude and the select group of wisdom-seekers. Indeed, it is complained that the subversive character of the literary and historical criticism which has preceded is due entirely to the acceptance of certain philosophical tenets which control the scientific activity and prejudice its direction. Although the statement is entirely inaccurate—for those purely scientific positions and their defences are compelling daily acceptance by their inherent weight—it illustrates the importance which attaches to the philosophical activity of the nineteenth century in view of the advance of Rationalism.

So far is it from true that all Rationalistic critics are controlled by a sceptical philosophy, that a large number of them still cling to Theism, or some attenuated shade of Theism, only in virtue of philosophical considerations. Thus Kuenen, one of the most iconoclastic of higher critics, was a devout Theist, and even Professor Max Müller, the most powerful advocate of the mythical theory of all theological doctrine, retains a belief in a supreme Reason in the physical and in the moral order. There is a curious irony of history in this fact. Religious belief preceded philosophy by countless ages, and has remained independent of its support until a comparatively recent date. Such religious belief, founded only upon a credulous acceptance of tradition, is at last rapidly decaying in civilized communities, and religion is concentrating itself upon certain broad philosophical considerations as its only enduring support. Philosophy is, as it were, an afterthought of believers. It did not bring religion into existence, yet it is somehow hoped that it will avail to prolong that existence when other sources of vitality are exhausted. Long before Thales had initiated the long train of thought that culminated in Plato and Aristotle religion had flourished in Greece, and it continued to sway the popular mind quite independently of the rise and fall of systems. With the wider diffusion of education, however, and the multiplication of every kind of literature, the necessity of a philosophic basis for religious belief is frankly recognised. Though the unthinking masses still continue, as they did twenty thousand years ago, to accept without question the myths and legends which their priests impress upon them, the number of those who demur to such curiously servile acceptance has grown enormous. Hence, not only is there a wide tendency to fall back upon fundamental Theistic positions before the advance of literary and historical criticism, but it is also clearly recognised that those fundamental positions —the existence of God and the nature of the human soul— must be logically established before there can be any question of entertaining a supposed revelation from God to the human soul. It is the duty of philosophy alone to establish those positions. The vicissitudes, therefore, of the philosophical world are of the first importance in estimating the contest between Rationalism and religious tradition.

History repeats itself perhaps more truly in philosophy than in any other branch of human affairs. In other sciences, at least, the mere secular accumulation of experiences ensures some progress in the course of ages; but the purely speculative character of philosophy makes a circular movement possible. We are certainly not advanced beyond the position of the philosophical world in Greece twenty-three centuries ago. A series of profound thinkers, grouped more or less distinctly into schools, had produced all the systems of thought which it is possible to produce on the problem. Materialism and Idealism, Monism and Dualism, Empiricism and Transcendentalism, had successively struggled from the seventh to the fourth century. Then came a natural relaxation into the weary scepticism of the immediate pre-Socratic school. In the interests of morality, Socrates and Plato lent all their genius to the resuscitation of dogmatism, and Aristotle imparted to it the utmost of purely logical strength of which it is susceptible; but it relapsed once more into the scepticism of the Neo-Academics and Neo-Peripatetics. The philosophical history of the last century and a half is a curious parallel to that brilliant Greek period, and its issue is a not dissimilar collapse. Transcendentalists will, of course, claim that certain elements, at least, of Kantism or Hegelianism are permanent acquisitions; but even Eclecticism, such as Victor Cousin advocated, is an utter failure. There is no important element of any purely philosophical system (*i.e.*, apart from certain physico-philosophical theories) which would be recognised with any approach to unanimity to be permanent. Our thinkers have but rung the changes on the old views of Xenophanes and Parmenides, of Leucippus and Democritus, of Pythagoras, and Zeno, and Plato, and Aristotle, and they have largely ended in the abyss of Gorgias and Protagoras, or of Pyrrho or Arcesilaus or Carneades. Germany's cynical abandonment of philosophy, to which the closing pages of Erdmann's history bear eloquent witness, after a century of amazing productiveness, is an impressive warning. France is in little better condition; England does little but fan the expiring embers of German systems—almost extinct in the land of their birth.

It would be impossible here to summarize the many systems that have reigned in the philosophical world during the present century; and, in fact, it is unnecessary for our purpose. Philosophy is a science of so comprehensive a range that innumerable issues are raised of a purely speculative character which have no power to affect the religious or social life of humanity. Here it will be sufficient to discuss philosophical controversies and estimate their issues in the bearing which they have upon religious tradition.

We have said that there is a tendency at the present time to sacrifice particular dogmas and symbols, and retreat upon the final positions of belief in God and an immortal soul, and an ethical relation of the two, which should be independent of historical records. Such a tendency has always been evinced by great and comparatively independent Christian thinkers (such as Descartes and Leibnitz), but it is now extended to a very large section of educated believers. These positions, which it is hoped to retain after the fall of traditional authority, are the two main problems of metaphysics. How do they stand after the keen struggle of antagonistic systems which has at length comparatively subsided? That is the only aspect of philosophic activity which interests the Rationalist as such. The problem of Realism *versus* Idealism is, to a great extent, connected with it; such problems as the nature of time or space may be conveniently disregarded. But on the fundamental problems of the nature and origin of man and of the existence of God, the strongest and keenest minds of all countries, enriched with the thought of all ages, have laboured throughout the century. What is the verdict of this last decade of the century?

It may be stated briefly that, at the commencement of the century, orthodoxy in philosophy was represented by the Scotch school of Reid and Dugald Stewart—the only comprehensive system at that time in England. Rationalism was represented by the empirical philosophy. To these was soon added the Transcendental philosophy imported from Germany by Coleridge and De Quincey. The Scotch system has struggled manfully throughout, being defended and developed by the powerful Sir William Hamilton, Dean Mansel, and a few minor lights. Kantism and Hegelianism have divided with it the allegiance of theologizing philosophers; Platonism, also revived by Coleridge, has likewise found many adherents. Empiricism, fully developed into a complete antagonism to traditional Theism, has had a stupendous growth, and has propagated religious scepticism far and wide in one or other of the forms it has assumed in the hands of Mill, Spencer, and Huxley. The interesting revival of scholasticism by a small and feeble group of Roman Catholic scholars, and the irritating opposition of muddle-headed Protestant divines who think theology can afford to be indifferent to the vicissitudes of philosophy, call for little mention. This catalogue of names, however, requires some amplification.

The empirical philosophy which has been the characteristic weapon of the English sceptics of the nineteenth century may be said to date from the time of Locke. There is no finality in speaking of the birth of systems; still it was in Locke's "Essay on the Human Understanding," published in 1690, that the principles of Sensism, or Sensationalism, or Empiricism, were first clearly enunciated. Locke himself was halting and inconsistent in the application of his declared principles; nevertheless, he was truly the "father" of recent British philosophy. His object was "to inquire into the origin, certainty, and extent of human knowledge, together with the grounds and degrees of belief, opinion, and assent." Hitherto philosophers had laboured and disputed upon different objects of human knowledge. Locke commenced the modern inquiry, more critical and more fundamental, into the nature, origin, and value of knowledge itself. The distinction had always been recognised between the mind, intellect, or intelligence, and the senses, and it had been thought that the mind had certain ideas or intuitions which had not come through the senses, whence most of our knowledge is obviously derived. Locke maintained that *all* our knowledge came through the senses; the mind was a mere *tabula rasa*, which received sense-impressions, combined and grouped them. The destructive consequences of such a system are apparent when it is known that the structure of proof which supports the theorems of the existence of God and the spirituality of the soul really rests upon those innate ideas or intuitions. Locke, however, did not pursue his principles so far; he remained a Theist. The system was little more than a revival of the principles of the Ionic school, which had been dormant for two thousand years. It is called Empiricism, or Sensationalism, because it reduces all knowledge to sensations (and their combinations) or experience (*empeiria*).

The new system was taken in hand in the eighteenth century by Hume and Berkeley in England, and by Condillac in France. By the middle of the century Condillac had shown the true consequences of the empirical method, rejecting the hesitation and the reservations (as of the notion of substance) of Locke. Bishop Berkeley, on the other hand, had evolved a system of pure Idealism from it, refuting Materialism by denying the very existence of matter. Hume, however, in his "Treatise on Human Nature" in 1738, and in his later works, pointed out that the principles established by Locke compel us to reject the notion of spirit equally with the notion of matter. Locke had inconsistently and arbitrarily admitted an objective value to the idea of substance; it was a complex idea, formed from the sense-impressions, and therefore devoid of objective validity. We are logically reduced to a knowledge of the sense-impressions of which we are conscious, and cannot get beyond them. We know nothing of substance, either material or spiritual, and nothing of causality; all our knowledge is merely an acquaintance with phenomena and their inter-relations. The result is, of course, pure scepticism: we can know nothing either of God or of the origin and destiny of man and the world. Such is the empirical system which has been adopted, with individual variations, by the English philosophical Rationalists of the present century.

Hume's philosophy was adopted and enforced, at the commencement of the century, by James Mill and his friend, Jeremy Bentham. Bentham will be more particularly noticed in connection with ethical utilitarianism, and James Mill soon gave place to the more powerful and more commanding influence of his son, John Stuart Mill, one of the most imposing figures in the philosophical and ethical circles of the century. Like Hume, he holds that all our knowledge is simply a knowledge of phenomena or appearances, and even this knowledge is relative, and not absolute; we are precluded, by the very nature of our minds, from attaining to a knowledge of anything beyond. Our sensations and their associations are the unique source of all knowledge; innate ideas and non-sensuous intuitions must be rejected. Even those axiomatic and invincible convictions to which the *à priori* and intuitionalist school appealed against him are only the result of accumulated impressions; the ideas of two-and-two and of four are so constantly associated in our experience that the bond is practically inseverable. The vindication of this aspect of the empirical philosophy is Mill's enduring merit; so, also, is his codification of the laws of association of states of consciousness.

The fundamental antithesis of philosophy, mind and matter, or self and not-self, is similarly explained; the inter-association of phenomena, according to co-existence, succession, and likeness, results finally into their division into two great aggregates, and thus produces the duality of the self and the not-self. Yet Mill is not a pure nihilist like Hume; he makes a certain concession to realism. Behind the actual sensations, which are all we can tangibly grasp as they flash upon consciousness, he recognises a vast background of "permanent possibilities of sensation" out of which they seem to emerge. In the same way, he faintly recognises a substratum of our states of consciousness: mind is "a series of feelings, with a background of possibilities of feeling." This vague and unsatisfactory outline of mind and matter is, however, all we can discern beyond our actual states of consciousness. The anthropological problem remains insoluble, and the usual arguments for the existence of a First Cause are mere sophistry. He thinks the teleological argument, the discarded work of Paley, the only one with the faintest gleam of hope; and in his posthumous "Essays on Religion" he makes a painful effort to lend some support to Theism. His effort cannot do more than suggest the existence of a non-omnipotent God, whom no system would accept. Mill's system has had a very wide influence throughout the century.

The number of writers who have subscribed to and popularized the empirical philosophy is very great and very illustrious. Lewes, in his "Problems of Life and Mind," and in his History, entirely accepts the empirical principles and their sceptical conclusions, which are common both to the English school and to Comtism, which he favoured. Professor Alexander Bain, the philosophical chief of Aberdeen University, of whom James Ward writes that, "with the exception of Locke, perhaps no English writer has made equally important contributions to the science of mind," has strenuously propagated the system in his classical works on psychology. Professor Clifford has advanced along the lines of Empiricism to a frank Materialism. Professor Tyndall, less a metaphysician than a most distinguished physicist, has been similarly conducted to Materialism. Professor Huxley has adhered more closely to the doctrine of Hume, rejecting not only

Materialism, but also the attenuated realism of John Stuart Mill. Deprecating all dogmatism as inconsistent with the modest nature of our only reliable knowledge—a knowledge of states of consciousness—he has suggested the name of Agnosticism to indicate the attitude of empiricists before the great world-problems. Under that title must be ranged all the distinguished names which precede, as well as Mr. Herbert Spencer, the Positivists (so far in sympathy), the long list of great writers who are more familiar in connection with ethics and general criticism—Harriet Martineau, George Eliot, Sir J. F. Stephen, John Morley, Charles Darwin, etc.

The most powerful advocate of empiricism, however, and the author of the form which is now most widely accepted, is Mr. Herbert Spencer. To give the barest outline of Mr. Spencer's vast system, in which the great wealth of modern science is largely incorporated, and which treats every branch of human activity and every aspect of being, is far beyond our scope.* Biology, psychology, sociology, ethics, æsthetics, and pedagogics are treated by the eminent philosopher with an exhaustiveness, and withal a unity of principle, which has no parallel in English literature. The law of evolution which astronomers, geologists, and biologists had successively detected is made an object of profound speculation, formulated as a universal law, and pursued throughout the entire dynamics of the universe. But to the empirical principles, and the rejection of Spiritualism and Theism, which are common to all Agnostics and Positivists, Mr. Spencer adds certain elements of a distinctive nature, which are usually regarded as an approach in the direction of Theism. Indeed, nothing is more common with German writers than to put him with or near Sir William Hamilton and Mr. Mansel. It is usually said that Mr. Spencer recognises with them the existence of an Absolute, and the entire inscrutability of its nature to human reason. The former, however, contends that we have no other source of knowledge of the Absolute, hence

---

* A comprehensive exposition of the system, written on the authority of Mr. Spencer, by F. H. Collins, under the title "Epitome of the Synthetic Philosophy," is an excellent introduction to Mr. Spencer's voluminous works.

it must remain for ever unknown and unknowable; the two latter maintain that by faith we can attain to a knowledge of God, and so pass on into an acceptance of Christianity. Still, in admitting the existence of the Absolute, Mr. Spencer seems to go far beyond all other Agnostics. *An Absolute* is, he thinks, necessarily postulated in the admission of the relative; since, however, all our knowledge is relative, and the Absolute is, by the very force of terms, an idea that excludes all relation, we cannot get beyond the knowledge of an Unknown Cause and a Universal Power, which is at the base alike of all science and of all religion. In virtue of his admission of an Absolute and a First Cause, he is usually claimed as approaching to Theism. It would seem, however, that all Mr. Spencer says is quite as consistent with Materialism as with Theism; just as the scholastic arguments for a First Cause and a Necessary Being may lead to Materialism or to Theism. And in Mr. Spencer's case the direction of his reasoning seems to be Materialistic throughout. Instead of his Agnosticism being considered as a halt on the way to Theism, it would more correctly be regarded as a halt on the way to Materialism. The Unknown and Unknowable source of phenomena may, metaphysically, just as well be matter as God; scientifically, the former alternative is simpler, and presents less difficulty. Mr. Spencer also departs from the Idealism of Hume and Huxley, and calls himself a "Transfigured Realist." He recognises an underlying support of our states of consciousness and an objective cause—a self and not-self; but they remain entirely inscrutable in their nature.

With the Agnostic school must be mentioned the Positivists, who are often, though inaccurately, confounded with them. From our present point of view, however, the two systems may be aptly associated. Auguste Comte, whose system has been widely adopted by French sceptics, starts from the empirical principles which we have described in the English school. All our knowledge is relative, and is confined to phenomena and their relations; to the inner essences, origins, and destinies of things we can never penetrate, and causes we know only as close associations of phenomena. Thus far the system is identical with the English system, and leads to the same Agnosticism in face of the higher problems. It differs in rejecting the introspective method in psychology, which it makes a branch of physiology, and in substituting for traditional religion a cult of humanity as the *Grand Être*, with saints, festivals, sacraments, etc. The latter is its chief offence in English eyes, and has elicited Mr. Huxley's caustic definition of Positivism, "Catholicism minus Christianity." Comte's philosophy was early introduced to English readers by Lewes and Harriet Martineau. It is now strenuously advocated, and finds many adherents through the distinguished historian, Frederic Harrison; Bridges, Beesley, and Congreve are also ardent Comtists.

In France the system has occupied the important position which Agnosticism has held in England; it has been the most important instrument in the spread of religious scepticism. In France, too, there has been much dogmatic Materialism; the line taken by Cabanis has been upheld by a number of physicians, such as Pinel, Broussais, Gall, etc. Another school, which held for a time a middle position between the theologians and the empiricists, was the Eclectic school, which was founded by Victor Cousin. It purported to select the better elements from the philosophies of Plato, Reid, Kant, and Hegel. Such an amalgamation could never be perfect, and it would perhaps be more accurate to describe them as stages in Cousin's development. He is rightly classed as Pantheistic, for the German element conspicuously preponderated in his Eclecticism. It was the official school in France for a time after the July revolution, and numbered many distinguished adherents—Royer Collard, Maine de Biran, Jouffroy, Prevost, Ancilla, etc.: Paul Janet, Jules Simon, and E. Caro are often aggregated to it. Another system which was yet nearer to orthodoxy, but was condemned by the Catholic Church, was Traditionalism. In varying degrees its followers held that reason was incapable of attaining the solution of the world-problems, and that authority or tradition is the only reliable guide in supra-sensible matters. J. de Maistre, Fraysinnous, De Bonald, and De Lamennais were traditionalists.

To return to England, from which both French Empiricists and Eclectics had largely borrowed, it must be said that the principal opponent of the rapid progress of Agnosticism was the Scotch school, which had inspired Royer Collard and Cousin. In the first half of the century, at least, the struggle lies between the followers of Mill and the followers of Sir William Hamilton. Here, again, the change of attitude of the opponents of Rationalism is deeply significant. The dogmatic intuitionalism of the old schoolmen, who were at least consistently logical and rational, has given place to a system which can only oppose "faith" to scepticism; the attempt to give a demonstrative solution of the world-problem is practically abandoned. Thomas Reid, the founder of the Scotch school, or school of "Common Sense," was alarmed at the sceptical results of the acceptance of Locke's principles. In his "Inquiry into the Human Mind with Principles of Common Sense," published in 1763, he introduces the new form of intuitionalism. He admits that Berkeley's and Hume's inferences are correct, and pleads that they form a *reductio ad absurdum* on the empirical principles. The empirical method in general must be retained; pneumatology will make no progress unless, like somatology, it runs on empirical lines. But the "ideal" system, as he calls it—the notion that we get all our ideas from without, and only come to judge about things by combining them—is incorrect. We must be admitted to have certain primitive judgments independently of experience, and "the sum-total of primitive judgments which are present in the consciousness of all men, and on which all certainty ultimately rests, is called common sense." How are we assured of the objective truth of such judgments? By an instinctive impulse to form them, a blind faith—not unlike the sentimentalism which had been advocated in Germany against the Rationalists. "It was," says Falckenberg, "a transfer of the innate faculty of judgment inculcated by the ethical and æsthetical writers from the practical to the theoretical field." Reid was immediately supported by Oswald and Dugald Stewart, and a number of minor writers. Whewell and Hamilton, though much influenced by Kant, subscribed to the principles of Reid; and the tradition has been ably supported in more recent times by Dean Mansel, and by Professor Fraser, Professor Veitch, Professor Spencer Baynes: Dr. McCosh and Dr. Cairns also adopt it with modifications. Hamilton (in whom and Mill the antagonistic forces were personified during the first half of the century) bases his philosophy on the facts of consciousness; but, in opposition to the passive receptivity of the Empirics, he emphasizes the mental activity of discrimination and judgment. At the same time, our knowledge is wholly relative, and cannot attain the unrelated; the Absolute is, therefore, inaccessible to our knowledge, and can be reached only by faith. Masson says of him that, "when affirming some cardinal belief from the logical demonstration of which he was precluded by his metaphysical Agnosticism, he was wont to say: 'If this is not so, God is a deceiver, and the root of our being a lie.'" Mansel attracted the suspicious attention of his clerical brethren by his advocacy of the relativity of our knowledge and our utter incompetency to reach the Unconditioned intellectually; at the same time, he incurred a severe attack from Mill for combining with this frank intellectual Agnosticism the elaborate Christian description of the Deity. Thus it is rather among Protestant divines than in the Roman Catholic Church (contrary to a very wide impression) that we meet the opposition of faith and reason. Catholic philosophers entirely condemn the criterion of the Scotch school. Hamiltonianism was also vigorously attacked by Ferrier, who takes an Idealistic standpoint. Dr. J. Martineau and a few other isolated thinkers have endeavoured to support Theistic positions on the more traditional arguments; but the majority of orthodox philosophers have either adopted some form of Hamiltonianism, or have accepted the teaching of Kant or Hegel. In the second half of the century the struggle lies chiefly between Spencerism and Kantism or Hegelianism (or a combination of the two), hence something must be said of the German philosophy.

To describe the series of philosophical systems which were put forward in Germany from Kant to Von Hartmann and Feuerbach would be a long and fruitless task. Kant was aroused, by Hume's idea of causality, to a train of thought which took form in the famous "Critique of Pure Reason" in 1781, and the "Critique of Practical Reason" in 1788. The empirical school had rejected the time-honoured distinction between sense and intellect. Kant, founding the transcendental school, retained it, and contended for an *à priori* element in thought, and even in sensibility. Time and space he thought to be structural habits or forms of the inner and outer sense. The categories, the notions of existence and non-existence, unity, causality, etc., were forms of the intellect, anterior to all sensation. Reason, the supreme faculty, had also "a structural relation to the three boundless yet necessarily-asserted objects—the World, the Soul, and God." But the characteristic feature of the transcendental system is that it deprives these supra-sensible forms and faculties of all objective value; only our sensations (and they denuded of their time and space elements) relate us to an objective world. Our ideas are only of objective value, in so far as they embody sense-elements, and the supreme synthesis into the World, Soul, and God is a purely subjective operation. Hence the agreement of the great German and English schools, in view of a rational solution of the world-problems, is obvious. Indeed, many eminent writers deprecate the supposed opposition between the two systems, and point out that the Germans have investigated the *nature* of knowledge, while the Empiricists have discussed its *origin*. Both agree that our knowledge is reduced to a knowledge of phenomena—the noumenon, the "thing-in-itself," is inaccessible to pure reason. Substance and cause are subjective notions—problems of origin, destiny, etc., are insoluble. But Kant's philosophy has been largely adopted in Theistic circles in virtue of a sort of appendix which appeared in the "Critique of Practical Reason." After demolishing every form of Theistic argument, Kant suddenly discovers that the practical reason (moral sense) brings us into relation with God and immortality. The objective value which he had refused to speculative principles is granted to the moral principles, and the moral law postulates a supreme Legislator and a sanction in a future life. That portion of Kant's system will claim attention later on.

An immediate disciple of Kant's, J. G. Fichte, developed his system as Hume had developed Locke's. He produced an idealistic and egoistic Pantheism. He thought Kant inconsistent in granting objectivity to sense-impressions and moral principles, and denying it to the categories. He consistently rejected the world of phenomena as well as the world of noumena, and was reduced to a subjective Idealism—the ego is the Absolute, the non-ego its subjective creation. Fichte was quickly followed by Schelling, who retains his Pantheism, but rejects his Idealism. His philosophy was rather a return to the Pantheism of Spinoza. Both Fichte and Schelling were, however, immediately eclipsed by Hegel, whose system prevailed throughout Germany in the early part of the century, and is very prevalent to-day in England, whither, it is said, "all good German systems go when they die." The fundamental problem of all theories of knowledge is the relation between thought and being. Kant had ended his critical campaign in what Fichte thought an inconsistent dualism. Fichte himself had removed being from the problem altogether. Schelling had identified them *in* the Absolute. Hegel identified them in themselves. The foundation principle in his system is the identity of the idea of being and the idea of nothing. Both are forms of the combining idea of becoming, and every thought is a poise between the two contradictories. Thus the laws of thought are also the laws of being. Logic is Metaphysics. "The true reality is unseen; all being is the embodiment of a pregnant thought, all becoming a movement of the concept; the world is a development of thought. The Absolute or the logical Idea exists first as a system of extra-mundane concepts, then it descends into the unconscious sphere of nature, awakens to self-consciousness in man, realizes its content in social institutions, in order, finally in art, religion, and science, to return to itself enriched and completed—*i.e.*, to attain a higher absoluteness than that of the beginning."[*] Hegel's system is certainly Pantheistic, but it is neither realistic nor idealistic; it has cut the Gordian knot.

The transcendental philosophy was introduced into England as a means of resisting empiricism at the beginning of the century by Coleridge and Wordsworth. Carlyle has been perhaps its most energetic supporter, though it is rather its influence that we find in him than a formal acceptance of the systems. J. H. Sterling was the first advocate of Hegelianism. In more recent times some form of Neo-Kantism or Neo-Hegelianism has found a large number of eminent supporters. T. H. Green, F. H. Bradley, J. Caird, E. Caird, J. P. Mahaffy, B. Bosanquet, Haldane, and many others, are mentioned as more or less faithful disciples of German teaching. The parallel between the

[*] R. Falckenberg, "History of Modern Philosophy."

ethical Theism of Plato and Kant is obvious, and hence it is natural to find that Plato and Kant are equally revered by the majority of the writers mentioned.

In Germany itself, while there has been so great a development of history and criticism, there has been a conspicuous decay of philosophy. A speaker at Hegel's grave predicted that his kingdom would be divided among his satraps, and certainly within a short period of his death his system was very generally abandoned. With the decay of metaphysics and the triumphant progress of physics, a powerful Materialistic school made its appearance; Feuerbach, Strauss, Dubois Raymond, Vogt, Lange, Büchner, Helmholz, and many other popular writers, have propagated it very extensively. Schopenhauer's system found much posthumous veneration. Schopenhauer agreed with Kant in his subjective Idealism, but went on to teach the utter blindness and irrationality of the world-ground in its despairing necessary evolution; hence the well-known pessimism of his school. Schopenhauer's philosophical inspirers had been Kant, Plato, and Buddha; the latter he is said to have venerated principally as an Atheist. The Oriental influence in his system is conspicuous. Hartmann's "Philosophy of the Unconscious" also received a moderate support. It was a compound of the thoughts of Hegel and Schopenhauer—the pessimism of the latter occupying a prominent position. Hartmann thought that the world was so essentially evil and wretched that its non-existence would be preferable to its existence; hence the final goal of the world-evolution was the blissful Nirvana of non-existence. Many writers returned to the anti-monistic and anti-idealistic teaching of Herbart. Lotze, in particular, has exercised a wide influence in the reaction; his teaching is a compound of Herbartian and Fichteo-Hegelian elements, and raises a strong protest against scientific Materialism.

Such, therefore, is the history of the rise, conflict, and decay of systems in the nineteenth century. The same painful impression is felt in surveying the drama, for such it truly is, as in surveying the Greek activity from Thales to Carneades. The most gifted minds of the three most gifted nations of modern Europe have sought, in grim earnest, a solution of the ever-impending problem of the universe; yet it can hardly be claimed that any positive advance has been made in the direction of a solution—certainly no constructive system bids fair to endure save in the history of philosophy. That there has been incidental profit from the ceaseless efforts of the various schools is beyond question. The science of psychology has derived enduring advantage. The work of Fechner, Wundt, etc., and of our own eminent English psychologists, Sully, Bain, etc., is certainly not of an ephemeral character. Yet even this brings us no nearer to the all-absorbing questions of anthropology—the nature and the destiny of the mind. One point, indeed, of some importance has secured a very general acceptance—the theory of a division of the possible objects of perception into noumena and phenomena, and the complementary doctrine of the phenomenal character of all our perceptions. The distinction is claimed to be Platonic in origin, though Plato's clear distinction into objects of sense and objects of mind (*nous*) can hardly be said to coincide accurately with Kant's. However, both Transcendentalists, Empiricists, and Hamiltonians agree in accepting the distinction, and it is pointed to as a permanent acquisition to metaphysics. Yet even here the opposition of the scientific Materialists must be included in the estimate; a system that numbers Tyndall, Clifford, Maudsley, Bastian, Draper, Pinet, Broussais, Moleschott, Helmholz, Büchner, Vogt, Feuerbach, and Strauss cannot be set aside as a negligeable quantity. Whether the distinction into noumena and phenomena be Platonic or not, it is certainly Aristotelic; it corresponds with the distinction into substance and accidents which the Stagyrite fully developed, and which plays a conspicuous part in mediæval philosophy. Now, the tendency of modern science is to suppress the duality which the metaphysicians have created. The schoolmen went so far as to teach the absolute separability of accidents from substance (as the Catholic dogma of Transubstantiation seemed to demand); modern phenomenalists, teaching the cognoscibility of phenomena and the imperceptibility of noumena, do not seem to be far behind them. But one by one their phenomena—sounds, odours, colours, etc.—have been conclusively shown to be merely modes of the sonorous, odorous, or coloured body, only separable from it by an abstraction. Hence to the scientist it must seem just as perplexing to talk of perceiving colours, etc., and not coloured things, as to believe in a bundle of supernatural qualities without a substance. This is a question in which both physics and metaphysics are concerned; the metaphysical position cannot long remain unaffected by the progress of physics.

It is, therefore, difficult to point to any positive results of the philosophical activity of the century which are likely to abide. Fortunately, it is the negative results which are mainly interesting to the Rationalistic historian, and in this aspect a profound change has been effected. To summarize the result as clearly and effectively as possible, we shall consider the change only in connection with the existence of God and the nature of the mind. During the last century Theism was equally strong on both sides of the controversy; the struggle lay between pure Theism and Christianity. The present century has witnessed a very numerous defection of the most eminent scholars from the ranks of Theism, a most extensive diffusion of theoretical Agnosticism in all but the very lowest classes, a remarkable collapse of the dogmatic defence of all philosophical Theists, and a very general tendency to substitute vague moral and mystic considerations for the "proofs" which formerly supported the Theistic position. Such a result is one of the most important elements of the progress of Rationalism.

It is unnecessary to repeat the long list of great writers who have unreservedly abandoned Theism during the progress of the controversy. Of the many eminent names which have been mentioned, only John Stuart Mill commenced his career in a definite Agnostic position; all the others are seceders from one or other forms of Theism. Again, it is unnecessary to enlarge upon the extent of the spread of Agnosticism in the nation at large. The writings of Huxley, Spencer, Darwin, Lewes, Harrison, Tyndall, etc., have had an enormous circulation. The works of Spencer, Bain, Leslie Stephen, Karl Pearson, and Clifford have entered into the university programme. Every review has been incessantly utilized by them, and a number of minor periodicals of pronounced Rationalistic temper have conveyed their theories and criticisms. England and France are permeated throughout with the Agnostic results of the empirical philosophy. And when we pass from declared Agnostics, who admit no shade of Theism, to the wider circle of those who have lost faith in the personal

God of tradition, but cling to some undefined and intangible shadow of the lost God, the number of those who are affected by Rationalistic criticism increases enormously. Whether a man is still entitled to the name of Theist who believes in an Absolute (not even an absolute being), an Unconditioned, an Unconscious, or a stream-of-tendency-not-ourselves-making-for-righteousness, is a question of terminology; but that vast modern pantheon of umbratilous deities, the *manes* of the Olympian family, bears eloquent witness to the progress of Rationalism. Then the large number of those who accept Hegelianism must ·be considered; belief in Hegel and belief in a personal God cannot long co-exist. The Neo-Kantists, including, perhaps, the larger number of orthodox professors of philosophy, find an escape from scepticism, with Kant, in the moral order: their position must be relegated to a future chapter. The followers of Hamilton and Mansel compensate their intellectual losses by a generous indulgence of faith. There are, no doubt, a large number of minds who will continue to find a relief in that manner; but it may be questioned whether the spread of scientific training is not calculated to correct that tendency. In fine, the old *à priori* (in the current sense) arguments for Theism have fallen into disrepute. The Roman Catholic attempt to restore their credit, though ably represented by Dr. Ward and Dr. Mivart, has been a signal failure; they have not elicited the slightest sympathy outside their own sect, and have met important opposition within it. The theological argument has also apparently lost favour in philosophical circles; indeed, the larger scientific view of the world-process which we now have gives no inconsiderable weight to the disteleologists. The most recent apologetic efforts, the works of Balfour, Drummond, Kidd, and Mallock, which, however undeservedly, have attracted universal attention, show that the whole question now turns upon the ethical problem. The spread of Platonism and Kantism points to the same conclusion. If it can be shown that the moral law is purely humanitarian in origin and effect, and entirely independent of the Theistic hypothesis, the last support of that hypothesis totters; whether the Agnostic moralists have made good that contention will appear in the sixth chapter.

On the question of the spirituality of the soul and its separability from the body the result of the philosophical struggle is, perhaps, more definite. The traditional notion of a spiritual principle informing a material structure, acting independently of it in its higher powers, and substantially separable from it, is now not only destitute of scientific proof, but is negatived by all the evidence of psychology. There is a general practice of either having recourse to "revealed" documents for a solution of the anthropological problem, or of seeking a solution in the phenomena of ethical life. Of the value of the revealed documents we have already seen the decision of the Rationalistic critics. Of the second source of hope of personal immortality we must again forbear to speak until we have discussed the ethical progress of the nineteenth century. The scholastic arguments for the spirituality of the soul have once more collapsed, and modern scholastics are at utter variance with regard to their value. Other philosophers entirely neglect them. The spiritualistic position has also been deeply affected by the discovery of the evolution of man. The proof of the somatic evolution of man from the lower animals (which will be described in the next chapter) concentrated attention upon the psychical differences which seemed to mark him off. These were not found sufficiently strong to forbid the extension of the doctrine of evolution to his mental constitution. The problem has, therefore, become a question of revealed doctrine or of ethical consideration for the majority of philosophers. When we remember that at the close of the last century the existence of a personal God and the immortality of the human soul were scarcely called into question outside of the French school of Diderot, Lamettrie, Holbach, and Cabanis, and when we consider the universal diffusion of Empiricism (Agnostic or Positivistic or Materialistic) and of Pantheism—each of which systems excludes both beliefs—in England, France, Italy, and Germany, we have a correct idea of the progress of Rationalism in the province of philosophy.

Chapter V.

RELIGION AND SCIENCE.

The conflict between scientists and theologians, which began with the very birth of scientific research, has culminated in an acute struggle, and practically ended in the nineteenth century. Outside the Church of Rome, which persists in ignoring or distorting, for the edification of its Index-bound laity, the stages of scientific progress, it is generally recognised in educated circles that the many controversies which have filled the scientific literature of the century are practically settled.

Correctly speaking, of course, the entire movement of the Rationalists is a scientific movement. Theology, ethics, history, and philosophy all fall into the category of sciences. However, the name has been so familiarly appropriated to the group of empirical sciences, in the narrow sense of the term (for all useful science must be empirical), that the "conflict between science and religion" has come to be specifically applied to the group of controversies we are about to describe. Neither term is quite accurate, for "religion" now frequently receives a much wider interpretation, in which it cannot conflict with science, but is bound to make harmonious progress with it; however, the phrase is too familiar to need explanation. Setting apart, therefore, the historical, ethical, and metaphysical sciences which have united in a radical criticism of that form of traditional theism which is currently known as "religion," we shall consider the progress of the physical sciences, and these only in so far as they have entered into conflict with religion. Few will dispute that the positions held by physicists, astronomers, geologists, biologists, and anthropologists against the fervid attack of theologians have now passed into established facts or theories, and are beyond all reasonable scepticism; theological opposition to science, the most pernicious hindrance to the advance of knowledge for many centuries, stands hopelessly discredited.

To appreciate fully the effect of scientific progress, it is necessary to discriminate between natural and supernatural, or revealed, or positive religion. The latter is contained in certain sacred documents; the former is understood to be the collection of statements concerning God and the soul and their ethical relationship to which "unaided" reason is capable of attaining. After the light which literary and historical criticism has shed upon the origin and value of Scripture, the twentieth century will probably think little of the conflict of theologians and scientists. Had the "higher criticism" been developed in the eighteenth century, the nineteenth could not have witnessed that conflict. No one is now surprised that the Old Testament is full of scientific errors. The error of their theological predecessors in opposing science in the interests of Genesis or Job is frankly recognised by latter-day apologists, and it is, therefore, trusted that the conflict is at an end, and that traditional religion is placed beyond the influence of science in thus abandoning the plenary inspiration of its Scriptures. A discussion of the effect of scientific progress upon even natural religion will probably unsettle that confidence. Meanwhile a brief sketch of the conflict of science with revelation will show that the struggle has ended through the abandonment of the theological positions.

It is a curious fact that astronomy numbers less religious sceptics among its great students than any of the other physical sciences. Nevertheless, for many centuries astronomy has been in acute conflict with theologians, and it was the first science to wrest from them a recognition of their errors. The Old Testament had naturally embodied the astronomical views of the Egyptians and Babylonians. Hence Christianity (with a few eminent exceptions) held it as a sacred doctrine that the earth was a flat, level plain, the firmament a solid vault that spanned it, and that light and darkness were positive entities equally created by God. The hard-fought progress of astronomy had dissipated these notions, and forced theologians to reinterpret their texts long before the present century. The struggles of Columbus, of Magellan, of Galileo, had gradually introduced a saner view of the universe. Magellan's famous voyage in 1519 settled for ever the question of the Antipodes and of the rotundity of the earth. The labours of Copernicus, Galileo, and Kepler destroyed one of the most vigorously defended points of theological astronomy—the geocentric doctrine; though the farce of theological opposition was sustained even until the year 1822, when the cardinals of the Holy Inquisition kindly permitted "the printing and publication of works treating of the motion of the earth and the stability of the sun, in accordance with the general opinion of modern astronomers." The religious notion of comets and meteors as fireballs flung from the hand of God to scare a wicked world was exploded by the labours of Tycho, Kepler, Newton, Halley, and Clairaut. The analogous notion that ascribed lightning and other meteorological phenomena to an arbitrary divine or diabolical influence had been completely destroyed; the discovery by Franklin in 1752 of the true nature of the lightning flash, that had been placed in the hands of Jupiter and of Jehovah, completely wrecked the traditional view, and rescued a vast territory for science from the province of theology. Medical science had fought with theologians over the bodies of witches and of the possessed, and had substituted humane and scientific treatment of epilepsy, dementia, etc., for the repulsive practices which religion had inspired; epidemics, also, had been wrested from theologians and received scientific study and treatment, and the value of sanitation had come to be understood. Even chemistry had collided with current theological views and profoundly modified them, shedding a new light on the phenomena of magic and witchcraft which the theologian had solemnly regarded as pertaining to his province from time immemorial. All this had been effected before the commencement of the present century, and one would expect to find a modesty and caution in the anti-scientific writings of the theologians of the century in some proportion to the universal overthrow of their predecessors. Such, however, is far from being the case: "the darkest hour is that before the dawn." Less equipped with social and physical penalties to inflict, the theologians of this century have been no less conspicuous than their brethren who broke the brave spirit of Galileo for reckless opposition, arrogant dogmatism, and ultimate collapse.

The fiercest struggles of the century have centred upon the description of the animate and inanimate universe contained in the first page of Genesis. In point of fact, there are two versions of the creation in Genesis, one of which represents the work as occupying the Creator six days, and the other one day only. The variation, however, offers little latitude; if the narrative is to be read in a natural sense, it compels the belief that the universe came from the hand of the Creator practically in its present form. The contrary theory of the gradual evolution of the universe from a chaotic condition had arisen in Greece, had been favoured by Scotus Erigena and Giordano Bruno, and came at length towards the close of the eighteenth century to be placed on a sound scientific basis. Starting from some rudimentary theories of Newton and Descartes, Immanuel Kant, the great German philosopher, presented to the scientific world what is now known as the "nebular hypothesis;" the hypothesis was at once adopted by Laplace, the eminent French astronomer, supported by physical and mathematical reasoning, and imposed upon the acceptance of scientific men as the most probable mode in which our solar system had originated. Contrary to the traditional view, the new theory taught that the formation of our solar system alone had occupied millions of years; that planets and satellites were annular fragments cast off by a vast condensing and rotating nebula, of which the sun is the actual nucleus, still in process of condensation. Such a theory was in diametrical opposition to the Genesiac version, and "throughout the theological world," says Dr. White, "there was an outcry at once against 'Atheism,' and war raged fiercely." But the power of the Church had happily waned, and evidence was accumulated zealously by astronomers in favour of the new theory; to-day it is one of the most brilliant, instructive, and impregnable positions of astronomy. It has given physicists an admirable basis for an explanation of the solar expenditure of light and heat; it fully harmonizes with the movements, positions, configuration, and comparative consistency and temperature of the planets and their satellites; it is in perfect analogy with the nature of the stellar universe (to which it has been extended) which has been unveiled by more perfect telescopic and spectroscopic research. The discovery of true nebulæ, in every stage of condensation, following upon Fraunhofer and Draper's perfection of spectral analysis, and the beautifully illustrative experiments of Plateau with rotating globules of oil, have closed the controversy.

A new science, which assumed a definite form only at the beginning of this century—the science of geology—at once entered into vigorous conflict with theology over the Genesiac legend. From time immemorial the fossils which are found in even the most superficial rocks had excited keen curiosity and much curious speculation : they were variously regarded as the product of "a stone-making force," a "formative influence," a "lapidific juice," a "fatty matter set into a fermentation by heat," a "seminal air," and other equally lucid causes—sometimes they were thought "sports of nature," sometimes (even by the great Chateaubriand, and in the face of the true version of their origin) sports of the Almighty. The true theory, that they were the petrified remains of animals and plants of previous ages, was, of course, suggested, but denounced as anti-scriptural. Even in the middle of the eighteenth century, in enlightened France, the great Buffon was forced to print an ignominious recantation of his geological teaching. Geology, however, gained in strength, and continued to reveal the secular evolution of the crust of the earth and the true nature of its fossil remains. Yet so great was the opposition that little more than half a century ago geology was still denounced by ecclesiastical writers as "not a subject of lawful inquiry," as "a dark art," a "forbidden province," an "infernal artillery," etc.; and Christian scholars who favoured it were assailed as "infidels" and "impugners of the sacred record." When the absurdity of the older views of the nature of fossils had gained recognition, the idea that they were traces of the great "Deluge" was generally defended by theologians. Dr. Buckland, an eminent Christian geologist, held the Deluge theory as late as 1823 ; but he at length yielded to the overwhelming evidence of his adversaries. In 1830 appeared Lyell's famous "Principles of Geology," and Lyell and William Smith succeeded in removing the old semi-religious theory from the path of progress. In 1856 it was quietly omitted from the new edition of Horne's "Introduction to the Scriptures," which was the standard text-book of orthodoxy. In the Church of Rome and the Russo-Greek Church the diluvian theory persisted much longer (in perfect harmony with Catholic traditions); but no theologian now lends his support to it. The story of the six-days' creation was simultaneously abandoned. The time which must have elapsed between the first descent of water upon the cooled film of the shrinking planet and the appearance of man in the upper strata of the crust (to confine ourselves to geology) is incalculable: the various estimates of scientists, both thermo-dynamicists and geologists, are widely divergent, but no authority claims less than 15,000,000 years for the formation of the earth alone. The days of Genesis, therefore, became the subject of further vigorous speculation and pseudo-scientific activity. The theory that a long period closed by a cataclysm must be placed between the first verse of Genesis and the commencement of the "days" was followed by a theory that the days were long periods of time; then by the admission that the periods were not strictly consecutive, or that they were visions of Adam or of Noah; and finally by the theory that the chapter was merely a religious poem or allegory. To-day, after the floods of literature that have been poured out, and the fierce and prolonged resistance to the progress of a science which is of great service to humanity, it is quietly recognised that the famous first chapter of Genesis is an expurgated version, by the unknown Elohist, of a Babylonian myth with no title to respect.

But there was yet a third violent controversy over the Genesiac version of the origin of the universe. According to Genesis, God had created all animals and plants according to their kind. It became, therefore, the sacred belief of Christendom that God had immediately and distinctly created all the species of the animate world. St. Augustine, it is true, makes a vague suggestion of the opposite, the evolutionary, hypothesis, which had been clearly taught in more ancient philosophies and theologies. However that may be, the theological world was profoundly convinced of the immutability and distinct origin of species when Trevir-anus and Lamarck threw out the first scientific defences of the contrary hypothesis, to be followed immediately by Geoffroy Saint-Hilaire. At once biology was added to the number of the victims of theology. There was, however, a lull in the storm until Chambers published his semi-evolutionary "Vestiges of Creation" in 1844. Eight years afterwards Herbert Spencer published an essay in favour of evolution; and in 1858 Charles Darwin and Alfred Russel Wallace gave birth to a definite theory of evolution by natural selection. In 1859 Darwin published his "Origin of Species," and Spencer, Wallace, Huxley, Galton, Tylor, Lubbock, and Lewes in England, and a large number of equally distinguished authorities in France and Germany, followed up the attack. A shower of theological diatribes followed, led by Wilberforce in the *Quarterly Review* and Manning in the Catholic *Academia*; it was called "a brutal philosophy," an "attempt to dethrone God," a "jungle of fanciful assumption," a "huge imposture"—an eminent French prelate, the amiable Mgr. Ségur, said, referring to the doctrines of the Darwinists: "Their father is pride, their mother impurity, their offspring revolutions." From end to end of the Church (or Churches) the loudest artillery boomed. Science persevered: in 1864 Sir Charles Lyell, hitherto faithful, published his "Antiquity of Man," and seceded to the evolutionists; a few years later Huxley published his "Man's Place in Nature," and in 1871 appeared Darwin's "Descent of Man." The theological artillery continued, but a change of tactics was perceptible: a careful study of the Hebrew text was now supposed to permit a much broader interpretation than tradition had given. Darwinism was now rarely denounced as anti-scriptural, but as "an utterly unsupported hypothesis," as "reckless and unscientific." Broad Churchmen, like Kingsley and Farrar, spoke in favour of Darwin; Bishop Temple and others began to accept Darwinism and give it a teleological consecration: Mivart did the same for Roman Catholics: Darwin was buried in Westminster Abbey with a panegyric from Canon Farrar. There was still from time to time an erratic explosion in high circles: Carlyle, with his hybrid theism, railed at Darwin as an "apostle of dirt worship," and Whewell refused to admit a copy of "The Origin of Species" in the library of Trinity College, Cambridge. But the opposition has now almost subsided; only third-rate theologians, decaying statesmen, and lady-novelists still echo the dying cry. The origin of species by evolution (whatever factors of that evolution may be ultimately assigned) is an accepted and a luminous theory of science; the doctrine of special creations is abandoned. In our own days we have heard an Anglican bishop, in an important ecclesiastical assembly, eulogizing Charles Darwin as a thinker who had rendered high service to theology by his famous theory.

"Per varios casus, per tot discrimina rerum."

The doctrine of the immediate creation of man was much more distinctly taught in Genesis, and has, therefore, been defended with a greater tenacity by theologians. Even here, however, time has brought about a general acceptance of the scientific theory. Many of the arguments which established the law of evolution in the animal world retain their force in application to man. Thus there are certain rudimentary organs found in the human organism (such as the appendix vermiformis and the glandula pinealis), and a number of atrophied muscles, which very clearly point to a pre-human ancestry; they are certainly unintelligible if we suppose the actual organism to be a divine *chef d'œuvre*. The development of the impregnated human ovulum also follows the same course as that of the higher animals; it is a recapitulation of the course of the evolution of the animal kingdom. The evidence of ethnology, too, entirely points towards a continuity of development between anthropoid animals and the earliest men. Such facts, added to the natural presumption of man's origin, which is grounded on the already-proved universality of evolution, fully establish the theory of human evolution from a scientific point of view. Again, therefore, there has been a reform in hermeneutics, and it is generally admitted that Scripture places no obstacle in the way. The only serious opposition now is based on the wide psychological gulf which separates man from the "lower" animals; hence there is a tendency to admit that the *body* of man is the product of evolution, but the *soul* an immediate creation. Since, however, the systems of philosophy which are at present in vogue give little support (as we have seen) to the theory of a distinct and separate spiritual substance in man, the complete doctrine of man's evolution is now generally accepted as it is taught by the Rationalists.

With this controversy is naturally connected the question of the antiquity of the human race, on which also theologians have waged zealous war with ethnologists, archæologists, and historians. That the Old Testament contained a chronology from which the antiquity of the human race was deducible was firmly held until the middle of the present century. There were wide discrepancies in the chronologies of interpreters, but the average opinion assigned to man an antiquity of about 4,000 years B.C., and none allowed more than 6,000 B.C. Dr. J. Lightfoot, a Vice-Chancellor of Cambridge and an erudite divine, definitely placed the creation of Adam on the 23rd of October, 4004 B.C., at nine o'clock in the morning. Scaliger in the sixteenth century, Sir W. Raleigh in the seventeenth, and others had protested in vain; when Young, Champollion, and Rosellini began a scientific study of the Egyptian monuments in the present century theologians were convinced that Scripture did not allow much more than 6,000 years for the antiquity of man. Egyptologists, Mariette, Brugsch, Meyer, Flinders Petrie, and Sayce are agreed that Mena or Menes, the first Egyptian king mentioned on the monuments, reigned at least more than 5,000 years ago. And the monuments further reveal the fact that Egypt had then already attained a high degree of civilization; its social, political, and military condition, its arts and sciences, its language, point indubitably to an immense period of earlier development. In the Nile Valley pottery has been dug out at such a depth that, calculating the annual deposit of the river, authorities place their date at 11,000 years B.C. Other researches in the valleys of the Tigris and Euphrates, and the decipherment of the cuneiform inscriptions, show that similar civilizations existed at Babylon and Assyria more than 6,000 years ago; their development must have taken many thousands of years of previous time. Archæology took up the story where history and philology had been obliged to abandon it. In 1847 Boucher de Perthes initiated the serious study of the flint weapons and implements which had been discovered in great abundance. In 1864 appeared Lyell's "Antiquity of Man," and a great number of anthropologists were won over to the new view of man's great antiquity. A vigorous search was instituted in all parts of the world, and flint instruments and human remains were found in deposits of the whole of the Quaternary period, and, according to the majority of authorities, even in Tertiary deposits. However that may be, man was clearly proved to have existed during a period of which the Scriptural 6,000 or 7,000 years is but a fraction. There is no need to repeat the story. The "drum ecclesiastic" beat loudly until the evidence was overwhelming. To-day it is generally held that the Old Testament teaches nothing about the antiquity of the human race; and that, if it did, it has no scientific value.

Following the order of Genesis, we come next to the doctrine of the Fall of man, which has also been a stumbling-block in the path of science. In this case the obstinacy of theologians has been, and is, unusually stolid; the doctrine of the Fall is the logical foundation for the whole soteriology of the New Testament. The issue of the controversy is, therefore, less tangible. Broad Churchmen had, as we have seen, already practically abandoned the dogma; they, therefore, accept the statements of scientists unreservedly. In general it can only be said that there has been the usual blind and prejudiced opposition to scientific positions, and that theologians have been compelled finally to accept the statements they had combated, the dogma being vaguely safeguarded (to that feeble extent which a theologian requires) by its own retreat into the deepest mists of antiquity.

On the Genesiac version of the Fall we should have to admit that man commenced his career in a state of high perfection, from which he gradually degenerated, to rise again in modern civilization; also, that death, cruelty, suffering, etc., only entered into the universe at the Fall. The latter portion of the legend was too obviously discredited by the earliest evidence of palæontology; it was quite clear from the animal remains found that fierce strife, keen suffering, painful disease, and death had not only existed throughout the millions of years before man appeared, but that they had been most important factors in the development of species. About the middle of the present century the first and more important part of the dogma—the early descent of man from a high civilization—received a severe blow from the combined researches of anthropologists, ethnologists, and historians. The examination of the flint instruments we have mentioned not only proved from their geological position the vast antiquity of the human race, but also the lowly condition of those primitive specimens of humanity. Then prehistoric skulls and bones were found at Cronstadt (in 1835), at Düsseldorf (1856), at Cro Magnon, Solutré, Furfooz, Grenelle, etc., which were not only of a lowly type, but were of many different types and ages, and showed a clear upward tendency from the earlier to the later. The latter conclusion was confirmed by a chronological arrangement (on geological grounds) of the rude primitive implements; the earlier and deeper are proportionately ruder than the later. In the shell-beds of Denmark more polished instruments, and even the remains of domestic animals, appeared. In the peat beds of Scandinavia a transverse section revealed a picturesque proof of the gradual " ascent " of man; in the lowest layers, mingled with botanical remains of an extreme antiquity, were smooth stone implements; in the middle layer, also full of extinct botanical specimens, were bronze implements; in the upper strata were implements of iron.

In 1853 the lake-deposits of Switzerland yielded relics of a higher and later stage of development—leather, cloth, grains, etc. Here, too, a gradual improvement appears from the lower to the higher and later levels. It was noticed, too, that the earlier bronze implements imitated the later stone, a proof that the bronze *followed* the stone age. Similar proofs were discovered in all parts of the world. Mr. Southall had contended, in 1875, much to the gratification of timid consciences, that Egypt showed no traces of a development from a rude age. Its civilization had come immediately from God. In point of fact, flint instruments had already been discovered in Egypt in 1867 and 1872, and the later discoveries of '77, '78, and '81 put the evolution of Egyptian civilization beyond question. *Ex uno disce omnes.* At the same time, the researches of ethnologists were giving strong confirmation to the archæologists. Ethnology proved that many races still existed in a low stage of development, and that an arrangement of the races of the earth would give a complete picture of the history of humanity. Whately led an attack, arguing that no rude race ever did or could emerge of itself from barbarism. Tylor, Lubbock, and others, crushed his contention. The Duke of Argyll led a new attack, contending that the lowly races had degenerated. It was abundantly proved that, against the local examples of decline, the vast majority of facts point to universal progress;

that the conditions suggested by the Duke do not, of themselves, involve decline; that many of his conclusions were, scientifically, extremely improbable, if not impossible; and that simple facts could be opposed to a large number of his statements. Comparative philology and comparative mythology tell the same story of a general upward progress of humanity in its speech and legends and religions. History in all its branches confirmed the theory of the universal ascent of man. The history of art, of science, of social and political development, of ethics, of religion—all commence with the simple and proceed to the elaborate later forms. Thus a half-dozen sciences, all that could shed light on the past history of humanity, declared unequivocally that man had ascended from the rudest beginning, little removed from animal life, to the height of civilization. The record of the past which these sciences have composed is far from complete, yet it gives a clear account of the general course of development. There is no trace of an early civilization or a golden age; it is absolutely negatived. To suppose, as some still do, that every trace of the primitive "descent" of man has miraculously escaped notice, while traces of his "ascent" have been yielded so abundantly, is the reverse of scientific. And when we remember that the only authority on which such a theory is based is an antique cuneiform cylinder from which a Jewish writer copied the folk-lore of the Babylonians, its attractiveness is not enhanced. In any case, we have here another remarkable instance of a theological opposition to science ending in complete collapse.

Another controversy which has ended in the retreat of theologians is that of the universality of the Deluge. The puerility of the notion of housing representatives of all the species of the animal world in an ark of the dimensions of Noah's began to be recognised from the seventeenth century. The rude classification and narrow horizon of the early makers of the legend had naturally led them to think that the number of species was very limited. With the growth of zoology as a science, the number of species increased enormously. The ark which is described in Genesis would contain only a small fraction of the innumerable species known to modern science—to say nothing of the infinite difficulties of arrangement, provision, etc. The zoological distribution of animals presented a still more serious difficulty. With the limited geographical notions of former days, it was possible to imagine a diffusion of animal life after the deluge; but the voyages of Columbus, Vasco da Gama, Magellan, Vespucci, and other navigators, and the discovery of the distribution of animal races over Australia, America, the islands of the Pacific, etc., made the theory of a dispersion from one centre (and at so recent a date) scientifically untenable. It has been shown, too, that the animals found to-day in any given locality have a genetic relation to the fossil forms that are entombed beneath their feet. Geology, also, entirely negatived the idea of a great deluge, and even astronomy raised insuperable objections. The result is well known. First, the universality of the deluge was sacrificed; then its extent was restricted more and more until it reached a vanishing point. It is now tacitly relegated to the region of Babylonian myths. The Genesiac account of the Flood is one of the clearest transcriptions from the cuneiform inscriptions.

Comparative philology is another science which shared the invectives of, and was grievously hindered by, theologians in its early years. From the story of the tower of Babel, Christianity felt bound to hold that Hebrew was the primitive language, and that all others were derived from it by a divine confusion at Babel. The notion that Hebrew was the primitive language had been virtually destroyed by Leibnitz, by the Jesuit Hernas in the eighteenth century, and by the works of Adelung: theologians, however, still clung to the Babel legend. In 1784 the Asiatic Society of Calcutta was founded, and the study of Sanscrit began. One by one languages fell into their places in an orderly scheme of development. Hebrew was assigned a subordinate place in the Semitic group: the idea of a "confusion" of tongues was shown to be a natural supposition of the primitive mind, but wholly unscientific. The languages of India, Persia, and of the greater part of Europe show a clear and orderly descent from a common ancestor: the same was proved for the Semitic and other groups. Both speech and writing are shown to have been gradually developed—not revealed to Adam; and the variety of languages is evidently the result of long development, just like the variety of races. Of course the new science was hampered and its scholars insulted. In 1788 James Beattie declared the new science "degrading to our nature;" in 1804 Dr. Adam Clarke made severe strictures upon it. Until the middle of the nineteenth century, when the new science was already accepted definitely in Germany, English theologians and theologasters continued to ridicule and denounce comparative philology. Even in these latter days Mr. Gladstone, so commanding a statesman, so pitifully feeble in religion, has made, says Dr. White, "an assertion regarding the results of philology which no philologist of any standing could admit, and then escapes in a cloud of rhetoric after his well-known fashion." It may be ranked with Lord Salisbury's pleasantries on biological evolution, Mr. Balfour on naturalistic ethics, the Duke of Argyll on ethnology, and Miss Marie Corelli on atomism. However, to-day the evolutionary theory of language is accepted; the Babel theory is as dead as the deluge. The last ironical page in this chapter of controversy is more pitiful than in the case of the other Judæo-Babylonian myths. The translation of the original Babylonian myth by Oppert, Sayce, and Schrader, and its comparison with Genesis xi. 1–9, makes it clear that the "confusion of tongues" is not even Babylonian, but is due to a conscious or unconscious *jeu de mots* of the Hebrew transcriber. Bab-el means "Gate of God," and the tower of Babel would be so called as supporting an altar to the God (in the sky), besides serving astronomical purposes. But the Hebrew writer has mistaken it for the Hebrew word "to confound," and built his myth thereupon—with the help of a Hindu legend.

Finally, we must mention the struggle of science and theology over the Dead Sea. Scepticism with regard to the Scripture version of the fate of Lot's wife, and its explanation of the peculiar properties of the Dead Sea, had begun in the seventeenth century. In the eighteenth travellers began to ridicule the salt statue which was pointed out by guides as the salicized relic of Lot's wife, and to tone down the exaggerated descriptions of the Dead Sea which were current in Europe. In 1806 Ulrich Seetzen began the serious investigation of the Dead Sea. The fruit of the region, which vast numbers of common Christians (and many of their pastors) still believe to be fair to look upon, but full of ashes and uneatable, he found to be like the same species in other parts of the world; the water was not "black and sticky," but blue and transparent; there was no smoke arising from it, and no statue of salt. Lynch made a bold investigation in 1848, and others followed. Before long it was made clear that all the features of the region, zoological, physical, chemical, and geological, are perfectly natural, and exclude the theory of a cataclysm. Lot's wife had elicited theories from well-meaning divines for centuries. Leclerc had suggested that the shock had made her "as rigid as a statue." Eichhorn suggested that she had fallen into a stream of bitumen; Michaelis that her relatives had raised a monument of rock-salt to her memory; Friedrich that she fell into the sea, and the salt stiffened round her clothing, etc., etc. To-day it is well known that the pillars of salt which men have regarded awe-stricken for ages as the remains of the unfortunate female are blocks of salt which the rain has detached from the main mass; on the very picture of it given by Lynch, still a treasured ornament of Sunday-schools and vicarages, there are in the back-ground a number of similar "statues" in process of formation. The whole myth is now generally recognised (outside the Church of Rome) to have grown out of the peculiar but perfectly natural features of the region.

Among practical sciences of great value to humanity, even medicine has incurred the hostility of theologians. The supernaturalistic air which has ever been thrown about disease and cure was always a hindrance to science, and there has been frequent ecclesiastical opposition to the progress of anatomy, medicine, and surgery; but after the fierce struggle of the anatomist, Vesalius, the opposition gradually languished. At the commencement of the present century the new practice of inoculation against small-pox was struggling with ecclesiastical prejudice; it was denounced as "an encroachment on the prerogatives of Jehovah," as "a sinful practice," as "bidding defiance to Heaven." Several Primitive Methodist ministers of a later date have opposed compulsory vaccination on theological grounds, and in the Roman Church the opposition was long violently maintained. During the great outbreak of small-pox in Canada (Montreal) in 1885 hundreds of Catholic lives were lost through the opposition of their priests to vaccination;

they declaimed against it from their pulpits in the midst of the plague, recommending, instead, rosaries and scapulars, and proclaiming that the hideous disease had been sent by Jehovah to punish them for their one glad, unecclesiastical festival—the Carnival. Happily, it is said that the episode has planted germs of scepticism in Catholic Canada which will never be eradicated. The theological opposition to the use of anæsthetics, especially in parturition, lasted until the middle of this century; women were denied the relief of anæsthetics in the awful pangs of child-birth (they were even burnt alive in olden days for having used them) because Genesis taught those pangs to be a legitimate curse from Jehovah. Hypnotism has met with keen theological opposition, for it has brought whole categories of "miracles" within the domain of science; it was violently denounced on that ground by the cathedral-preacher of Augsburg as late as 1888.

Lastly, we may instance the science of political economy as one that has been grievously hindered by Scriptural teaching. Both in the Old and New Testaments the loan of money at interest is condemned. On the other hand, it was soon discovered in the progress of commerce that such loans were not only a matter of great convenience, but of absolute necessity. For many centuries the commercial world was oppressed by this ecclesiastical stricture; fathers, popes, and councils sternly prohibiting all interest on money. The policy was firmly imbedded in canon law, and was vigorously followed out by clergy and authorities. The result was that, says Dr. White, "the whole evolution of European civilization was greatly hindered," and the practice of money-lending was confined to the Jews; being certainly damned already, the latter lost little by practising it— though, after driving the Jews from every other industry and restricting money-lending to them, it is hard that the Church should now inspire anti-Semitic movements. By the middle of the eighteenth century the ecclesiastical policy, certainly based on Scripture as it was, had become intolerable, and theologians began to retreat. Benedict XIV., in 1745, decreed that usury (which he took to be synonymous with interest) was a sin, but might be permissible in certain conditions; and in 1830 Mastrofini issued an authorized work in which he contended that the Church only condemned *exorbitant* interest. Yet, even in 1830, the Inquisition would not commit itself on the principle, and many priests and professors still hurled anathemas at the practice. In 1872 the Holy Office calmly sanctioned the practice; and, according to M. Zola, the present occupant of the Holy See derives a large income from the practice—a significant commentary on the stern denunciations of Leo the Great, Urban III., Alexander III., Gregory IX., Gregory X., Clement V., Leo X., and Innocent XI. The ethical teaching of the Papacy is immutable indeed!

When we compare the present accepted view of the origin of Genesis with the fierce and prolonged resistance which theologians offered to scientific progress, a feeling of profound pity is inevitably experienced. On the authority of a collection of folk-stories, which Jewish writers translated into their own language and foisted upon Moses, the progress of modern science has been barred with preternatural hostility in every single direction. Not a line of inquiry into the nature of past or present has been started, but the way has been sternly blocked, "By Order, Moses," and scientists have had to waste valuable energy in repelling the ceaseless attacks of theologians with their little-understood legends. Men of high character and genius—Copernicus, Apion, Galileo, Newton, Linnæus, Buffon, Cuvier, Agassiz, Maillet, Gosse—have been forced into silence, inactivity, subterfuges, shameful withdrawals for the protection of those legends. Science and civilization, with their attendant blessings, have been hindered for centuries; scientists of noble and benevolent life have been persecuted, calumniated, accused of the basest possible motives; a vast fund of energy has been squandered and withdrawn from the service of humanity; the most useful discoveries and inventions—the lightning rod vaccination, anæsthetics, hypnotism, even railways and telegraphs, etc.—have been opposed and anathematized, all in virtue of the Jewish translation of certain Babylonian and other myths.

But it is hoped that the conflict is now ended for ever. The Protestant Church is generally convinced that no scientific statements must be sought in Scripture. The Church of Rome will express a like conviction as soon as its present despot, who is, like Gladstone or Manning, an eminent statesman, but an uncritical and impermeable scholar, has been replaced. The era of struggle will then be over, it is thought, and the provinces of science and of theology clearly distinguished. But it would seem that the significance of scientific teaching is felt, not only in connection with Scripture, but in connection with pure theism or natural religion. The mere fact that science has come into violent conflict with the sacred books of Christianity, and proved them to be in error, does not help us to understand why most of the eminent scientists of this century have passed into utter religious scepticism. The rejection of the Bible leads logically only to Deism. Nineteenth-century science, it is proverbial, leads to Agnosticism—to a monistic and mechanical conception of the universe rather than the older dualism. Let us endeavour to show how the modern scientific view of the universe, based on the results of a hundred sciences, has had such influence in this dissolution of theism and spiritualism.

And first it is well to note how fully the old view of the macrocosm harmonized with ethico-theistic teaching. Even after the overthrow of geocentricism, although the arrangement of the heavenly bodies became a little less natural, still the earth was easily realized to be the true centre of the universe. It was still a narrow and well-ordered universe, limited in time and space. Within, all lines seem to converge to the earth; without, the illimitable void suggested an encircling Immensity; and, before and after, the mind could only place the eternal life of God. On earth, too, first the very presence of life, then the endless variety of living things, and finally the pre-eminent power and nobility of man, seemed to point to an extra-mundane Artificer. Thus the best conception of the cosmos obtainable before the nineteenth century was conspicuously incomplete. Its *lacunæ* seemed to be harmoniously filled up by philosophy and religion. And, given the spirituality of man and the existence of God, the moral law, still veiled in mysticism, pointed naturally towards immortality. In a word, the revolution may be said to consist in this: that the limits of time and space have been swept away, the *lacunæ* or gaps in the fabric of the universe have been almost filled up, the moral law has been scientifically studied and placed on a new foundation. Naturally the supplementary (as one may call them) hypotheses of spiritualism and theism have been proportionately superseded.

In the first place, the horizon of the human mind has receded with each successive generation. It was soon found that our solar system, instead of being the centre of a group of brilliant but comparatively insignificant stars, set like golden lamps in a firmament that hemmed in the narrow world, was merely one member of a vast cluster of solar systems. The solid firmament was a figment of imagination; the sphere of attenuated matter which casts the blue light upon the earth could, it is said, be conveniently packed in a hand-bag. The stars are not glowing particles of incorruptible matter, but huge incandescent suns, 3,000,000 or more miles in girth, disseminated throughout space at such unimaginable distances that only the faintest glimmering of their light falls upon our retina. More than 100,000,000 of them are revealed by the telescope, most of them larger than the sun (which is 130,000 times larger than the earth); and the photographic plate reveals further millions incalculable. Apparently void spaces in the heavens are shown, by a plate exposed ten or eleven hours, to be absolutely crowded with worlds. Trigonometry shows that they are at incalculable distances from us and from one another: the nearest is 25 billion miles away—Arcturus is at a distance of 1,500 billion miles. Indeed, since the spectroscope has revealed that they are rushing at terrific speed through space, some at 250 miles per second, their infinite dispersion is necessary. All these worlds form a vast annular system, of which our solar system is a modest member; though order is not perfect—Arcturus and others obey no law of harmonious motion, and collisions are not unknown. Nor is our idea of the vastness of the universe limited here. Other stellar universes are thought to be perceived—the great Andromeda nebula is probably one at a distance of six million billion miles at least. In fine, the old space-limits have entirely vanished; every increase of instrumental range reveals new worlds—we have no warrant for putting limits to the cosmos.

The more startling revelation is the discovery of the vast antiquity of the universe. Geology claims millions of years for the solidification of the earth; astronomy demands yet further millions for the evolution of the solar system from its primitive nebula. Nor is this all. Astronomy has discovered numerous extinct suns, much larger than ours—such as the satellite of Algol and stars of that type, the half-extinct companion of Sirius, etc. For their evolution a still longer period is necessary; the vista of time extends as indefinitely as the vista of space. In fact, astronomy unveils this panorama to our gaze. The universe, as far as we see it, is a collection of vast masses of matter in every stage of condensation—from the dark solid Algol star to the flocculent nebula in Orion. Condensation implies age, for the more solid bodies are the result of a secular condensation of attenuated nebulæ. Dark stars are numerous, how numerous it is impossible to say from the nature of the case; and nebulae are found in thousands. Hence we must think that the great universe lived, as it now lives, ages before our solar system was born, and will live on ages indefinite after our sun and all planetary life are extinct. It is a vast procession of worlds, a drama of birth and life and death, of which science sees no beginning and no end, and has not the slightest reason to suspect either. Take the nebula in Orion: in the triangular space apparently cut out of it is a cluster of stars. It is impossible to resist the inference that they have been formed by condensation from the nebula: the thought that the rest of the great nebula will similarly condense into worlds opens out a dazing vista of futurity. Take, again, the cluster of more than 2,000 stars, called the Pleiades—more than 1,000 billion miles away. The wisps and faint wreaths of nebulous matter that still enwrap the vast cluster make us think that the whole group is a crystallization of a vast primitive nebula, and thus open out an equally unimaginable vista of past time. Worlds are being born, are in the prime of life, are burning down, and are quite extinct everywhere around us. Our sun happens to have just passed its prime. It has no prerogatives in the vast host of the heavens. Thus have all limits of time and space been swept away, and the bases of that imaginative vision of an encircling Infinity and Eternity been destroyed. The world now points to no past, no future, and no infinity but its own.

In the third place, science has undermined the theory that it is necessary to postulate a supreme Architect who formed the actual cosmos from the primeval chaos. All the supposed proofs of a supreme wisdom in assigning the positions, regulating the motions, etc., of the heavenly bodies have entirely collapsed. Every feature of the actual orderly universe is a direct and inevitable result of the inherent properties of the original nebula. So far was "chaos" from needing a "Logos" to direct its growth into a "cosmos" —in other words, so little did the nebula need a Designer —that it could not have evolved in any other direction: the law of gravitation determined all in advance. The word "law" is but an abstract way of regarding the action of force, and science has every reason to think that force is only matter in motion. Thus science has beaten back the "watch-maker" argument until it simply implies that matter and motion must have had a creator—in other words, teleology, as such, has vanished, or is only tacked on as an appendix to the argument for a First Cause. And, as we saw in the preceding chapter, modern philosophy, both empirical and transcendental, entirely rejects the causation argument.

Then, when we come to the great breaches in the hierarchy of being as it was conceived a century ago, we find that they have already been almost entirely filled up. Until a few centuries ago the doctrine of the spontaneous generation of living beings (from non-living) was universally admitted. Scientists proved that the supposed cases of abiogenesis were fallacious, and that in no actual case is life born from non-life. The facile and erratic mind of the theologian immediately erected this empirical statement into an *à priori* dogma: it is still quite common to read in sacro-scientific literature that the researches of Pasteur, etc., have proved the *impossibility* of the birth of life from inanimate matter. Science, it need not be said, does not lay down *à priori* dogmas, and in this case it furnishes ample data for the opinion that life was evolved from non-life. The perfection of the microscope has opened out fields of living things which were hitherto undreamed of. Apart from Pasteur's experiments, any scientist would now hesitate about thinking that such highly-organized creatures as the Infusoria could arise by abiogenesis—to say nothing of bees, frogs, etc. But when we come to such monocellular organisms as the Amœba, the case is very different. Little structureless atoms of protoplasm, there is little faith involved in thinking they arose spontaneously: put one side by side with a white corpuscle of the blood in the microscope, and one might almost lose their identity. We have no reason for thinking that they are ever produced by abiogenesis to-day; but to say that they *could not* be, and, especially, that they cannot have been so produced in the unimaginable physical conditions of the early palæozoic period, would be absurd. In fact, there may have been yet simpler forms of life, and a substance or substances between ordinary matter and protoplasm—in the earliest strata all traces are naturally destroyed. Moreover, chemistry has succeeded in forming artificially a number of organic substances—alcohol, indigo, uric acid, etc. In such favourable conditions, therefore, the law of evolution, uniform in action up to this point and beyond it, demands the admission of the commencement of life by abiogenesis: even Catholic scientists accept the position. Thus is the first great gulf bridged over.

With regard to the connection of the infinite variety of plant and animal forms which stood out as distinct creations a century ago, it is unnecessary to say much. Palæontology has supplied valuable intermediate forms and linked disparate species, and has connected the species living in a given region with their fossil predecessors. Embryology has shown that each ovulum recapitulates in its development the history of the species to which the parent belongs. Anatomy has discovered rudimentary organs (like the teeth of the whale, etc.) that refer to former species. Zoology has added a mass of evidence which cannot here be condensed. However, the thesis that all the species have arisen by evolution is, as we have said, universally accepted, even blessed by ecclesiastics. This continuity is completely proved until we come to man, and science affords no basis for the theory of an extra-mundane and non-mechanical interference. As Caro politely expressed it: "Science has conducted God to its frontiers, and thanked him for his provisional services."

As we saw above, there has been a more ardent struggle against the extension of evolutionary principles to man. In accordance with traditional views, a distinction has been drawn between mind and body. With regard to his corporeal frame, there is no longer a serious resistance to the evolutionary doctrine. The evidence of embryology and of comparative anatomy is more than adequate for scientific proof that man has descended or ascended from another animal species. Then comparative psychology has done much towards bridging the gulf between the mind of man and that of other animals. The mental powers of the higher animals have been carefully studied (for the first time) on the one hand by Darwin, Romanes, Lubbock, etc., and the mental powers of the lowest races of men on the other; and a close *rapprochement*, if not satisfactory evidence of continuity, has been the result. In the meantime, the old psychology, the scholastic psychology, which mistook a superficial for a radical and specific difference, and thus erected an *à priori* barrier to the transition, has lost favour. Modern psychology is an empirical science that refuses to dogmatize about the "spirituality" of the soul. Hence no metaphysical objection can be raised to the development of man from another animal species, and the whole weight of the law of evolution, absolutely proved up to this point, and most strongly corroborated by anatomy, embryology, comparative psychology, and ethnology, teaches that development. Only a vague mysticism, taking the form of certain "extra-rational" considerations, is opposed to the scientific view. The doctrine is strongly re-inforced by the discovery of the action of evolution in every department of human activity—in art, in science, in religion, in morality, in sociology, in language. At no point is there a breach of continuity by an extra-mundane intervention. All the alleged historical interventions have been dissolved into myths and legends.

It will be now apparent that science has a powerful influence upon religion* quite apart from its positive mythology. The cardinal points of every religious scheme are the existence of a personal God, and the distinctive spirituality of the human mind or soul. Science builds up such a conception of the universe and its contents as

* We are aware that the term "religion" is retained by many Agnostics, who understand by that name the principle of reverence for all that is high and ideal in life. It is evident we are not using the term in that sense, but as an equivalent of theism or theology; and by "God" (theos) we mean exclusively the Personal God of Christianity and Judaism.

tends to exclude those beliefs. Any belief in things invisible, if it is more than a subjective illusion as vain as a dream, must be founded on things visible. It must have the character of an inference from the defects or deficiency of the scientific view of the universe. The modern scientific picture of the cosmos is too complete and too harmonious to justify such an inference. Human life is not now a field of light surrounded by an infinite mystery—a unique drama on the central stage of the universe. It is a bubble on the stream of time that flows on indefinitely before and after; a chance episode in the play of force on the bosom of a material immensity. A nebula, one of the countless myriads that people space, condensed and formed a sun with a retinue of planets. The planet Terra has reached that stage of consistency and temperature at which life is possible, and in the ceaseless play of force life expands and is perfected, and reaches the higher levels of human art and science and sociology. The conditions of life, water, atmosphere, etc., will gradually vanish, and the episode of human life be ended. The moon has undergone such an evolution. The Earth, Venus, and Mars appear to be at about the same stage of it; the larger planets are considerably less advanced. It is a question of magnitude *versus* the inevitable force of gravitation. Myriads uncounted of similar histories are being enacted in every region of space. Extinct stars prolong the story deep into the unthinkable past, and giant nebulæ point to its indefinite futurity. The cosmos is one vast self-containing mechanism, complete and self-sufficient, unaffected by any agency save its own physical interaction, with no suspicion of a beginning or an end. Unless ethics opens out, as Kant thought it did, a glimpse into another world, there is not only no basis for belief in such a world, but there is strong counter-proof. Once it is admitted that there is no tangible positive proof of the existence of God, there are certain features of life, hitherto considered a mystery, which tend to positively exclude that belief. The main instruments of the long evolution of life, the incessant conflict, the cruel and bloody struggle, the disease and pain and famine and suffering of every form, from the very dawn of consciousness; and the pitiful spectacle of human life in particular, the thousands of years of degradation, of misery, of hideous brutality and suffering, of stupid impotence, of the triumph of all that is evil and loathsome—all that Schopenhauer and Von Hartmann so eloquently pleaded—return in intenser force against the theistic hypothesis. It can no longer be said that theism is a purely open question like "lunar politics." We do but rid ourselves of a painful mystery in rejecting it.

That the mechanical theory of the universe is not free from mysteries only a too sanguine Materialist would deny. The formation of the first living organisms is yet beyond the reach of hypothesis, and the rise of consciousness and its relation to cerebral change is a still profounder mystery. To decline to accept the theory, however, on the ground that it does not explain everything, would be a surprising attitude for the adherents of a religious system which is conspicuous for the number and obscurity of its mysteries. The human race will await many ages longer, and, perhaps, never obtain an exhaustive theory of the universe. At the same time, the vast progress which science has already accomplished, and the number of obscurities it has already illumined since the days of Bacon and Galileo, give ample ground for hope. On the other hand, the very hypotheses which would be introduced by dualists really increase the mystery, while giving a superficial explanation. The notions of a spiritual soul, of a supreme Designer, and of a Moral Legislator, give no real explanation of the phenomena of thought, of cosmic order, and of morality: they are no more satisfactory than the "aquosity" that once explained the formation of water, or the "lapidific force" that explained fossils. We can conceive no way of connecting them with the phenomena they are introduced to explain; and they bring in additional mysteries in abundance. However that may be, it is not a question of calculating which system contains least mystery; it is a question of fact. That matter exists we know: the idealistic criticisms of Mr. Balfour and others may be safely disregarded, for the slightest serious concession to idealism at once paralyses and stultifies all philosophic discussion, and throws us into a Fichtean egoism. That spirit exists we have no further reason for thinking, now that science has embraced the whole cosmos in its mechanical and evolutionary scheme. Thus reasoned Dr. Tyndall, Dr. Clifford, and a large proportion of the most eminent scientists of the present century. Thus it is that science bears a direct relation to the permanent elements of religion, and not only to its sacred documents: the continued progress of science means an extension of its mechanical formulæ, and the ultimate suppression of mysticism and spiritualism. In this way it reacts constantly on religious philosophy, and, through philosophy, on religion.

Chapter VI.

RATIONALISM IN ETHICS: CONSTRUCTIVE RATIONALISM.

Surprise is often expressed that certain writers, who seem to accept some of the most advanced Rationalistic doctrines, cling, nevertheless, to the Theistic system which modern Rationalism has, as a body, abandoned. Thus we have seen, in the first chapter, that a large section or members and divines of the Established Church have so far yielded to the dissolving forces of the age as to abandon some of the most prominent dogmas of Christianity. Instead, however, of taking up an independent position, they make a determined effort, and finally succeed in enlarging the boundaries of the Church, modifying its legislation and entirely eviscerating its formulæ, and thus remain nominal members and hold high positions in the Anglican communion. The same circumstance appears in the region of philosophy. The clash of systems, and the depth to which metaphysical criticism has penetrated, have produced a general scepticism with regard to the ontological features of older schools. Yet there is a large number of thinkers who shrink from the position of avowed unbelief, and who make interesting efforts to provide a new basis for reasonable acceptance of Theism. The recent attempt of Mr. Balfour to substitute a vague and glorified authority for logical processes, and the laboured analogical reasoning of Drummond, are well-known instances.

In all these cases we have the operation of one and the same idea. Christianity has fused religion and morality so intimately that it is feared the fall of traditional religion would lead to a contemptuous disregard of the moral law, which would have very serious consequences to society. Morality has become juridical and wholly theistic, instead of the independent tradition it once was. If the seal of divinity be removed from it in the popular esteem, there are many who think that there is no authority adequate to enforce its dictates. This apprehension was openly expressed by the Coleridgean school, as we have seen. The Church, to them, was an institution for the purification of life and the enforcement of moral discipline, and they sought to defend it on that ground only. Philosophical sceptics, from Kant to A. Balfour, have clung to Theism on the same principle. They think that the moral law would survive in the minds of a few grave and high-principled scholars, but would soon be trampled under the feet of the multitude if the supernatural halo were to depart from it. Kant himself, of course, cannot be placed in the same category with the later sceptics. He did not profess to establish a theism on the assumed evil consequences of Agnosticism, but to pass, by direct reasoning, from moral phenomena to a moral legislator and a necessary sanction in immortality, though there are many who accept Heine's version of the matter, which would put Kant in the same position as later moralists. However, there are several writers of the present day who take their stand definitely on the supposed moral or immoral consequences of Rationalism. Balfour and Mallock, for instance, evince a thorough scepticism on all speculative Theistic defence, yet advocate the retention of Theistic belief on the ground that its rejection would have serious practical consequences. The more advanced Broad-Churchmen—Dr. Momerie, A. Craufurd, etc.—are evidently in the same predicament. The large number of clergymen and professors who accept Kantism or Hegelianism, or that interesting combination of the two which is sometimes called Transcendentalism, must join on the same issue. In fact, it is not too much to say that the main issue between Theists and Agnostics is now an ethical issue. There are few, indeed, at the present day who would venture to support Theistic belief by direct metaphysical arguments; between empiricism and transcendentalism metaphysics has been wholly discredited. A certain number still find a divine glow on the universe at large, marks of design and wisdom, etc.; but their perception is only capable, apparently, of being thrown into the form of "extra-rational" considerations. The majority of Theists base their belief upon ethical considerations.

It has been pointed out by Rationalists, in the first place, that the reasoning of such apologists as Mr. Balfour and Mr. Mallock assumes a fund of stupidity on the part of the "vulgus," about whose moral fate they are anxious, which can hardly be admitted. An argument founded solely upon the unsatisfactory results of "naturalism" would hardly satisfy even our very easily-satisfied *bourgeoisie*. To say that there is no speculative proof that God exists, but that the moral law will not be reverenced unless people believe he does, is a reasonable position to take up. But to go on to infer that he *does* exist, because of these evil consequences of disbelief, is a curious intellectual feat, though the argument is not a discovery of Mr. Balfour's; it is many centuries old in scholastic authors. The people at large would soon perceive this Theism of their anxious philosophers to be a *fictio juris*, no less than a trick to keep them moral, and would quickly nullify it. Unless, therefore, the Theist argues as Kant and Newman do—that is, that the moral law speculatively considered as a phenomenon points to the existence of God—his reasoning will not stand the test of time. On this point it is that the history of the operations of Rationalists in the domain of ethics is of profound importance, and we proceed at once to its narration. It will be impossible to give a full description of the ethical systems which have appeared during the century. We confine ourselves to those features of them which are most relevant to the main thesis of the progress of Rationalism.

The nineteenth century closes the Deistic controversy, and opens with the struggle between the new Rationalism, empirical Agnosticism, and the orthodox theologians. In ethics the Rationalists oppose utilitarianism to orthodox juridical morality. The germs of the new system are, as usual, discovered in the old Greek controversies. Socrates, rising in an age of universal scepticism, and sceptical himself on most speculative questions, even on the immortality of the soul, made a vigorous stand for moral tradition. From Socrates sprang two widely-divergent ethical schools, the Cyrenaic and the Stoic. Aristippus, the leader of the Cyrenaics, taught that the end of moral action, the only criterion of the morality of acts, was the pleasure of the moment and of the individual. His egoistic hedonism was, in fact, little more than a philosophical defence of self-indulgence, sophistically evolved from the teaching of Socrates. At a later date the system of hedonism (the theory that pleasure or happiness—"hedone"—is the end of moral action) was adopted by Epicurus, who, however, removed its sensualistic features, embracing the higher social and intellectual enjoyments under the title of pleasure. This is the system which has served as a basis for modern Rationalistic systems, hence we omit other ethical schools. Christianity, in the meantime, introduced, or gave more prominence to, the idea of *law* and of moral *obligation.*

About the year 1650 Hobbes attempted, in two treatises, to revive interest in Epicurus, and rehabilitated his egoistic hedonism. Locke, remaining a Theist and intuitionist with regard to ethical principles, gives his assent to both the egoistic and the hedonistic features of the system. Hume, the real founder of modern Utilitarianism, defines virtue as a quality approved by spectators, and finds that only those qualities are approved which are useful and agreeable. He maintains that "reason is no motive to action" (against the Platonists who attacked Hobbes), and that there is no obligation to virtue except such as arises from the agent's own interest or happiness. Paley also adopted Utilitarian principles. He decides moral questions, and determines moral obligation, chiefly by appreciating the tendency of actions to promote or diminish the general happiness. In his esteem, of course, this whole Utilitarian system is of divine ordination.

Thus it is that, at the commencement of the century, we find Bentham and James Mill upholding an universalistic hedonism or utilitarianism against the Intuitionists and Theists. The passage, however, from egoism to altruism or universalism was strongly contested by Bentham's opponents (the Scotch school, and, after a time, the Græco-Germans led by Coleridge), and was indifferently defended by him. When pressed, he was obliged to admit that the only interests which a man is at all times sure to find adequate motives for consulting are his own. He was wont to say that "nothing but a self-regarding affection will serve for diet, though, for a dessert, benevolence is a very valuable addition." The work of subsequent

Agnostic moralists is precisely the elucidation and strengthening of this passage from individual to general welfare, so as to give security and permanency to the moral code. Of Bentham's immediate followers, Austin seems to have returned to the position of Paley. Grote extenuates the claim of the general interest upon the individual by considering duty as practically limited by reciprocity. John Stuart Mill continues the orderly development of the Utilitarian theory.

In J. S. Mill's system we find an unqualified subordination of individual to general welfare. It is, in fact, an Epicureanism strengthened by Stoical elements, and by ideas borrowed from Comtism. In his essay on "Utilitarianism," published in 1861, Mill is chiefly occupied in defending the system from the objections of sensualism and selfishness which the earlier presentations of it have excited. He differs from Bentham in establishing a distinction in kind between different orders of pleasures, and contending that the pleasures of the higher kind (although they may be less intense) must be preferred to the lower as ends of action. In this, however, which appears to be a fragment of pure Stoicism without an argumentative basis, Mill is generally deserted by later Utilitarians as inconsistent with hedonistic principles. He makes the higher principle which classifies pleasures, rather than pleasure itself, the basis of moral preference. Then, in further distinction from Bentham, he maintains that a disinterested public spirit should be the principal ground both for the performance of socially useful work, and for the inculcation of hygienic principles. Hence he does not identify the moral sentiment (in so far as it is altruistic) with sympathy or benevolence. Virtue is to be loved as "a thing desirable in itself." At the same time, he is forced to admit that, as Sidgwick expresses it, "the function of moral censure (including self-censure), as distinct from moral praise, should be restricted to the prevention of conduct that positively harms others, or impedes their pursuit of their own happiness, or violates engagements expressly or tacitly undertaken by the agent." He has then to explain the logical basis of his altruism, always the principal point of attack from anti-Utilitarians, and to lend it a support which would appeal to the unphilosophical multitude as effectively as Theistic threats and promises. Here Mill makes a distinct advance in the work of construction. The moral sentiment has arisen, he maintains, partly through artificial and partly through natural causes. The artificial influence, the "education of conscience under government or authority," tends to yield to the "dissolving force of analysis." The natural causes of the altruistic moral sense are the "social feelings of mankind," which are a complex blending of (1) sympathy with the pleasures and pains of others, and (2) the habit of consulting the welfare of others from a consciousness of mutual need and implication of interests. On the latter point Mill evidently touches the sociological argument which later scholars elaborated. This feeling of unity with one's fellows engenders a "natural want" in any "properly-cultivated moral nature" to be in harmony with others, though he admits that some are devoid of it and ethically hopeless. In the course of time, the objects which were originally desired only as means to an end come, through the laws of association, to be directly pleasant and desirable; hence his apparently Stoical maxim, that virtue must be loved as a thing desirable in itself. He contends, also, that the acquired tendency to virtuous conduct may grow so strong as to persist even when there is not only no pleasure to be gained by it, but quite the reverse. Thus, Utilitarian morality is as capable of producing moral heroes as any other ethical system, and Mill's celebrated assertion, that he would go to hell rather than pay a mendacious compliment to the Deity, is much more in harmony with his teaching than Dr. Mivart or Mr. Mallock imagines. Dr. Bain's view of the origin of the moral sentiment is, broadly, similar to Mr. Mill's.

The chief argument against the Associational theory of moral feeling was based on the early age at which that feeling is manifested by children. This objection was met and answered by the next form which hedonism took—the evolutionary theory, which has now generally superseded the Associational. Not that there is a conflict between the consecutive schools of "naturalistic" ethics. It is a development parallel to that of Biblical criticism. Each new school supersedes its predecessor only in the sense that it introduces new elements, and is thus enabled to meet the old difficulties more effectively. The great crux of the hedonists had ever been the altruistic element, which is necessary in every system that seeks to uphold the traditional ethical code. This difficulty has been entirely surmounted in the evolutionary theory as it is presented by Mr. Leslie Stephen, the eminent Rationalistic critic, or by Mr. Herbert Spencer, the great Synthetic philosopher. Charles Darwin and W. K. Clifford are also earlier eminent exponents of the evolutionary theory. The new theory finds the incentive to altruism and the origin of the altruistic feeling in the social nature of man. Man is not an independent unit, whose actions happen to conflict with the interests of other independent units; but he is part of an organic whole, and half the pleasure of life is derived from that social connection. His actions are, therefore, directly and functionally related to his fellow-men, and to the integrity, health, and preservation of the organism into which he is incorporated. Altruism thus turns out to be an enlightened self-interest. The unthinking egoism of an Aristippus, or the anti-social individualism of a modern Nietzsche, are equally injurious to the individual himself in the ultimate analysis. He suffers with the depression of the social organism as inevitably as do the members of a diseased body. Morality is therefore, as Mr. Stephen says, " the definition of some of the most important qualities of the social organism." The bridge from egoism to universalism has been safely constructed.

Mr. Stephen, in his " Science of Ethics," accepts happiness (in a broader sense) as the ultimate end of reasonable conduct, but he rejects the Benthamite method of ascertaining empirically the conduciveness of actions to this end. He finds a more scientific criterion in their conduciveness to the " efficiency," for the purpose of its preservation, of the social organism (or social tissue, as he prefers to call it). He differs from Mr. Spencer in his estimate of the future, holding that sociology, which Mr. Spencer thinks sufficiently advanced to predict an ideal society, is as yet "nothing more than a collection of unverified guesses and vague generalities disguised under a more or less pretentious apparatus of quasi-scientific terminology." He does not, therefore, accept (few writers do) Mr. Spencer's distinction of absolute and relative ethics.

A few evolutionary writers think happiness or pleasure a

mere accompaniment of the "preservation" of society which is the end of moral action. Mr. Spencer, in his "Data of Ethics," dissents from them, and thinks that conduct tending to the preservation of life is only good on the express assumption that life is attended with a "surplus of agreeable feelings." Ethics, he thinks, is not primarily concerned with the actual condition of human beings, but with an ideal society in which normal conduct will produce "pleasure unalloyed by pain anywhere." In such a society, which Mr. Spencer feels justified in predicting, moral conduct will be spontaneous. Absolute ethics is thus concerned with this ideal state, and deduces from necessary principles what conditions must be detrimental and what conditions must be beneficial in an ideal society. Relative ethics is a provisionary science, determining how far these absolute rules are applicable to the actual condition of humanity. In any case, the empirical reasoning of the earlier Utilitarians, and the attempt to adjust the balance of pleasure and pain, have given place to a more scientific treatment. Moral rules are deduced from sociological laws. As Mr. Stephen says: "A full perception of the truth that society is not a mere aggregate, but an organic growth...... supplies the most characteristic postulate of modern speculation." The conceptions of modern biology are also utilized, especially by Herbert Spencer. Thus the difficulty of the early appearance of the moral sense in the child (a point which is much exaggerated) is met by the doctrine of transmission of parental characteristics by heredity. The long experience of the race has roughly determined which courses of action are prejudicial, and thus formed an empirical decalogue. These results are permanently registered on the nervous system, and transmitted with it in reproduction.

The older intuitive school of ethics, the school of Butler, Shaftesbury, Hutcheson, etc., which opposed the empirical school in the last century, has few followers in the modern controversy. Dr. J. Martineau is its most eminent representative. With it may be associated the Hamiltonians and the Catholic writers. Its decay is largely due to the introduction into England of the German systems, which have been generally adopted by the opponents of empiricism. Kant, as we saw previously, arrived at the conclusion that pure or speculative reason was wholly subjective in its operation, but declared the objective value of practical reason or conscience. His fundamental principle is that duty must be done for duty's sake, and the criterion for determining individual duty is : "Act according to that maxim (or subjective principle) alone which thou canst, at the same time, will to be a universal law." This "categorical imperative," or sense of obligation, implies the freedom of the will; "thou shalt" implies "thou canst." Thus the moral law convinces us of freedom, though, in reality, the moral law is simply the law of the will itself, and the will is free when acting under this law. From the sense of obligation he deduces also the existence of a Supreme Legislator, and the necessity for a future life in which morality will be adequately vindicated.

However, by the time that the English Broad-Churchmen had adopted Kantism it had been superseded in Germany by the teaching of Hegel. Hegel held with Kant "that duty or good conduct consists in the conscious realization of the free reasonable will which is essentially the same in all rational beings. But Kant's ethical principle, owing to his purely formal conception of reason itself, does not admit the connection he sought to give it with practical life. His followers attempt to remedy this by still basing morality in reason, but seeking its content and realization in practical life and its institutions. Hegel conceives the universal will as objectively presented to each man in the laws, institutions, and customary morality of the community (for he is both pantheist and evolutionist), not applied by a subjective principle, as Kant thought. If concience conflicts with the common sense of the community, it must be resisted. Conscientious individual effort is self-deceived and futile unless it attains its realization in harmony with the objective social relations in which the individual finds himself placed. A compound of the teaching of Kant and Hegel, such as is worked out by T. H. Green, is now usually received in England and Germany. In his "Prolegomena to Ethics," published in 1883, Green attempts a combination of the two. "The ultimate standard of worth," he says, "is an ideal of personal worth;" yet "it is equally true that the human spirit can only realize itself, or fulfil its idea, in persons, and that it can only do this through society, since society is the condition of the development of a personality." Caird, Bradley, Sorley, Mackenzie, and others, support some modified form of Hegelianism.

The two later German theorists, Schopenhauer and Von Hartmann, have proved, as a whole, unassimilable to the English mind, though their influence is felt. Schopenhauer, according to whom the world is due to an irrational act of unconscious will, productive of hopeless misery, thinks all true morality is summed up in the denial of will, (1) by the repression of egoism, by the practice of ordinary virtue, of love and sympathy; (2) by ascetic self-mortification (he was much influenced by Buddhism). Hartmann says we must aim at the negation of the "will to live" (the incurable source of evil), not each by himself, but collectively, by working towards the end of the world-process and the annihilation of all so-called existence. These systems are not unconnected with the literary pessimism which is often opposed to Mr. Spencer's sociological optimism.

If, therefore, we return to the question of "naturalism *versus* supernaturalism," as the prevailing controversy is sometimes, though inaccurately, called, we find that this great progress of Rationalistic ethics brings us nearer to a solution. The issue has been gradually contracted until it rests almost exclusively on the ethical problem. If morality can find a secure and permanent basis apart from Theistic belief, most of the defence of that belief which is put forward in modern times breaks down completely. Such a basis is clearly provided in the modern school of independent ethics. In the first place, recent moralists have given a more scientific analysis of morality and immorality than was formerly obtainable. The principle of ethical discrimination is not a new one. For many centuries in Catholic theology—the only systematic moral theology—the ethical criterion has been mainly utilitarian. All theologians admitted that morality or immorality was intrinsic to actions, and did not arise from a divine command or prohibition. Actions were not immoral because forbidden, but they were forbidden because they were immoral. And, in analyzing this inherent immorality of certain acts, it was generally traced to their social harmfulness, and conscience was declared to be reason practically applying that criterion. There was, however, always some confusion owing to the existence of a written moral code; and not infrequently divines, like Cardinal Newman, degenerated into an utterly mystic view of conscience and morality. The true criterion has now been disengaged from obscuring circumstances, and specific moral problems are more likely to find a solution. Then, with regard to the sanction of moral conduct, the principal point of anxiety, it is difficult to see how any serious apprehension can be felt about the transfer of ethics from a Theistic to a utilitarian basis. The belief that each immoral act was a breach of an arbitrary positive code, without any but penal consequences, which could be avoided with ridiculous facility by believers, has not proved a very effective safeguard of morality in the course of history. Only a keen personal faith could make it conspicuously effective. Such faith is rare in these latter days, and is certainly not likely to be nourished by modern Theistic apologies. On the other hand, a doctrine which points out that immoral acts, and especially the habits which they fatally induce, are profoundly injurious to the fabric of society, and tend to destroy the conditions of mutual confidence and honour and sympathy which lie at its foundations, seems to have legitimate hope of appealing to an age which is increasingly remarkable for humanitarianism and social endeavour, and appreciation of mutual dependence. Indeed, the very fears which are expressed by Balfour, Mallock, etc., do but confirm the position of the Utilitarians. They emphasize the fact that immorality has grave social consequences, and that the real basis of morality is utilitarian. Those consequences only need to be pointed out clearly and definitely to the popular intelligence, as they are present in the systematic thoughts of philosophers, and the basis is given for a new ethical training of more consistent character, and of more cogent appeal. It would be an unjustifiable pessimism to think that men are incapable of being educated to such a moral code.

It is now clear that the reproach which is frequently addressed to Rationalists—that they are purely destructive and iconoclastic—is entirely incorrect. All the great Rationalists of the present century—J. and J. S. Mill, Darwin,

Huxley, Harriet Martineau, George Eliot, Leslie Stephen, Spencer, Bain, Clifford—have co-operated in removing ethics to an independent basis, and have eloquently promulgated the new motives of morality in their works. They are convinced that morality will only be purified and elevated when moral acts are no longer performed for the sake of supernatural rewards, or out of fear of torment, and that men will be the more easily induced to lead consistently moral lives when they are taught to regard the moral law, not as an alien precept imposed by a tantalizing Deity, and in utter antagonism to self-interest, but as a rational adjustment of their own interests, the higher with the lower, and the individual impulses with the social obligations. And, under the influence of those great writers, a large number of ethical fellowships have already appeared, sustaining a high moral standard among all sections of the community on purely humanitarian grounds. The work is rapidly increasing, and finds ready converts in all classes of society. It is an object-lesson in constructive Rationalism, a practical answer to the timid apprehensions of wavering Theists, an anticipation of the purely secularistic moral training of the years to come.

Owing to the marvellous literary activity of the present age, the results which have been attained in the various departments of Rationalism have been immediately communicated to almost every class in the community. The scepticism of a Bayle or a Hobbes could be confined within very narrow limits, and even the criticism of Hume or of Voltaire had a comparatively limited audience. The enormous quantity and the graduated character of modern literature have had the effect of diffusing a reasoned scepticism in social strata which had been hitherto impermeable. Religious controversy of a fundamental character rages in all but the very lowest social spheres. The working man, who has neither leisure nor faculty to enter the labyrinthic details of the struggle, is nevertheless able to appreciate its broad moral. The mere continuance of the struggle and its ever-increasing difficulty naturally enfeeble his trust in traditional doctrine. Secularist and Christian Evidence lecturers are ever assailing him with their conflicting statements. He is but too ready to listen to the politician or sociologist who would divert his attention from the shadowy region of the unknown to the more acute and tangible interests of the present.

To the more educated the results of Rationalistic progress are unfailingly presented. The restless, apologetic tone which the ecclesiastical world has everywhere adopted is of itself an indication of the power and the wide diffusion of sceptical research. The eminent sceptics of the century—Darwin, Huxley, Mill, Tyndall, etc.—have appealed directly to the masses, and not merely to the cultured few. Their thoughts have been still further popularized by a number of Rationalistic periodicals, and by an infinity of publications emanating from less academic sources. And apart from the eminent scientists, such as Tyndall, Huxley, and Darwin; philosophers, such as Mill and Spencer; literary critics and historians, such as Stephen, Morley, Lecky, Harrison, Carlyle, Arnold, etc., who have propagated the spirit and the results of Rationalism so effectively, much has been done by writers in the lighter paths of literature. Innumerable poets have, in their verse, breathed the free, anti-dogmatic spirit of the age—Shelley, Clough, Tennyson, Browning, Matthew Arnold, George Eliot, George Meredith, Swinburne, and many others. In fiction also the Rationalistic spirit has found eloquent expression. George Eliot, Mrs. Lynn Linton, George Meredith, Thomas Hardy, Rudyard Kipling, Grant Allen, represent uncompromising scepticism. Mrs. Humphry Ward, Sarah Grand, Olive Schreiner, with a large number of male novelists, breathe a wholesome Rationalistic spirit, though they restrain its influence within a narrow sphere. In the leading reviews Rationalism has for a long time occupied a prominent position. During the second half of the century, at least, there is not a single impartial review or magazine which has not been continuously utilized by the most powerful Rationalistic critics. Even the daily papers have come at length to deal impartially with Rationalistic writers in their reviews of current literature. The literary influence of the vast and important body of sceptical writers of the century has proved overwhelming.

It is not surprising, therefore, to find changes in the legislature corresponding to this expansion of public opinion. The religious tests which had so long discredited the universities have been abolished. The substitution of a

Secular affirmation for an oath has been obtained by the strenuous advocacy of the late Mr. Charles Bradlaugh, Mr. G. J. Holyoake, and others. Even the laws which still remain on the Statute Book are no longer enforced in the tyrannical manner they were brought to bear in the earlier part of the century. In 1819 Richard Carlile was sentenced to three years' imprisonment and £1,500 fine for selling Paine's "Age of Reason"—merely a Deistic publication. Many other severe prosecutions followed for a similar offence, and most of the leading Secularist lecturers have suffered under the blasphemy laws. At the present day the most advanced literature is sold with impunity, and, though Mr. Foote and his colleagues have not sacrificed a tittle of the liberty of speech for which they suffered, the present generation would be startled at any revival of the blasphemy prosecutions. Still, there is much work yet to be done in removing the disabilities of Freethinkers. The grave injuries they are still liable to incur, for instance, with regard to trusts, or contracts, or custody of children, or Sunday lectures, etc., reflect deep disgrace upon our legislative machinery. They are the last relics of that sacerdotal tyranny which dreads discussion and continues to the last its policy of persecution.

Finally the development and secularization of education must be taken into account in estimating the growth of Rationalism in the present century. The State has taken upon itself the task of educating its children, which religious bodies had so grossly neglected until 1870. The great perfection of elementary education in recent years, together with the growing tendency to divorce it completely from religious instruction, has made millions of minds receptive to Rationalistic influence, which had hitherto been entirely beyond its reach. At the same time, the abolition of religious tests and the open profession of religious scepticism in higher educational spheres have facilitated progress. Many of the most fearless critics of the age have been and are professors at the leading universities; indeed, the proportion of Rationalists among the University professors who have attained lasting literary recognition is remarkably high. And the most important Rationalistic works and theories are freely taught and commented upon in all the great Universities.

Thus it is that the progress of the Rationalistic spirit must be estimated, not only by the novelty and solidity of its achievements, but also by the universality of its diffusion. The theories and discoveries we have summarized are not "idols of the den"—they are the possession of all ranks of society. The evening paper, the Sunday paper, the myriads of leaflets and cheap publications, and the voices of innumerable popular lecturers bear them incessantly to the labouring classes. The social and humanitarian movements which the time-spirit has evoked are largely characterized by a purely secular character, which contrasts ominously with earlier movements, and which is anxiously deprecated by theologians. Literature is almost universally secularistic—is very largely anti-dogmatic and anti-sacerdotal. Dogmatism is visibly decaying. The Church is appealing to æsthetic, or ethical, or humanitarian influences, and suffering an unrestrained license of thought in speculative regions. In fine, the progress of the Rationalistic spirit in this nineteenth century is indefinitely greater than during the entire eighteen centuries since the Galilean and his followers infused a new life into the Hebrew, Hindoo, and Egyptian versions of the primitive solar myths.

Printed for the Rationalist Press Committee by WATTS & CO., 17, Johnson's Court, Fleet Street, E.C.

31

www.ingramcontent.com/pod-product-compliance
Lightning Source LLC
Chambersburg PA
CBHW020313170426
43202CB00008B/589